# CHARACTER & OPINION

### IN THE

# UNITED STATES

## WITH REMINISCENCES OF
## WILLIAM JAMES AND JOSIAH ROYCE
## AND ACADEMIC LIFE IN AMERICA

BY

### GEORGE SANTAYANA
LATE PROFESSOR OF PHILOSOPHY IN HARVARD UNIVERSITY

LONDON
CONSTABLE AND COMPANY LTD.
1920

5866

6.88.

7

# PREFACE

THE major part of this book is composed of lectures originally addressed to British audiences. I have added a good deal, but I make no apology, now that the whole may fall under American eyes, for preserving the tone and attitude of a detached observer. Not at all on the ground that "to see ourselves as others see us" would be to see ourselves truly; on the contrary, I agree with Spinoza where he says that other people's idea of a man is apt to be a better expression of their nature than of his. I accept this principle in the present instance, and am willing it should be applied to the judgements contained in this book, in which the reader may see chiefly expressions of my own feelings and hints of my own opinions. Only an American—and I am not one except by long association [1]—can speak for the heart

[1] Perhaps I should add that I have not been in the United States since January 1912. My observations stretched, with some intervals, through the forty years preceding that date.

of America. I try to understand it, as a
family friend may who has a different temperament; but it is only my own mind that
I speak for at bottom, or wish to speak for.
Certainly my sentiments are of little importance compared with the volume and
destiny of the things I discuss here : yet the
critic and artist too have their rights, and to
take as calm and as long a view as possible
seems to be but another name for the love
of truth.  Moreover, I suspect that my feelings are secretly shared by many people in
America, natives and foreigners, who may
not have the courage or the occasion to
express them frankly.  After all, it has been
acquaintance with America and American
philosophers that has chiefly contributed to
clear and to settle my own mind.  I have no
axe to grind, only my thoughts to burnish,
in the hope that some part of the truth of
things may be reflected there ; and I am
confident of not giving serious offence to the
judicious, because they will feel that it is
affection for the American people that makes
me wish that what is best and most beautiful
should not be absent from their lives.

Civilisation is perhaps approaching one of

those long winters that overtake it from time
to time. A flood of barbarism from below
may soon level all the fair works of our
Christian ancestors, as another flood two
thousand years ago levelled those of the
ancients. Romantic Christendom — picturesque, passionate, unhappy episode—may be
coming to an end. Such a catastrophe would
be no reason for despair. Nothing lasts for
ever; but the elasticity of life is wonderful,
and even if the world lost its memory it could
not lose its youth. Under the deluge, and
watered by it, seeds of all sorts would survive
against the time to come, even if what might
eventually spring from them, under the new'
circumstances, should wear a strange aspect.
In a certain measure, and unintentionally,
both this destruction and this restoration
have already occurred in America. There is
much forgetfulness, much callow disrespect
for what is past or alien; but there is a fund
of vigour, goodness, and hope such as no
nation ever possessed before. In what sometimes looks like American greediness and
jostling for the front place, all is love of
achievement, nothing is unkindness; it is a
fearless people, and free from malice, as you

might see in their eyes and gestures, even if their conduct did not prove it. This soil is propitious to every seed, and tares must needs grow in it; but why should it not also breed clear thinking, honest judgement, and rational happiness ? These things are indeed not necessary to existence, and without them America might long remain rich and populous like many a barbarous land in the past; but in that case its existence would be hounded, like theirs, by falsity and remorse. May Heaven avert the omen, and make the new world a better world than the old ! In the classical and romantic tradition of Europe, love, of which there was very little, was supposed to be kindled by beauty, of which there was a great deal: perhaps moral chemistry may be able to reverse this operation, and in the future and in America it may breed beauty out of love.

# CONTENTS

## CHAPTER I

## CHAPTER II

## CHAPTER III

## CHAPTER IV

## CHAPTER V

## CHAPTER VI

## CHAPTER VII

# CHAPTER I

## THE MORAL BACKGROUND

ABOUT the middle of the nineteenth century, in the quiet sunshine of provincial prosperity, New England had an Indian summer of the mind; and an agreeable reflective literature showed how brilliant that russet and yellow season could be. There were poets, historians, orators, preachers, most of whom had studied foreign literatures and had travelled; they demurely kept up with the times; they were universal humanists. But it was all a harvest of leaves; these worthies had an expurgated and barren conception of life; theirs was the purity of sweet old age. Sometimes they made attempts to rejuvenate their minds by broaching native subjects; they wished to prove how much matter for poetry the new world supplied, and they wrote " Rip van Winkle," " Hia-

1                               B

watha," or "Evangeline"; but the inspiration did not seem much more American than that of Swift or Ossian or Châteaubriand. These cultivated writers lacked native roots and fresh sap because the American intellect itself lacked them. Their culture was half a pious survival, half an intentional acquirement; it was not the inevitable flowering of a fresh experience. Later there have been admirable analytic novelists who have depicted American life as it is, but rather bitterly, rather sadly; as if the joy and the illusion of it did not inspire them, but only an abstract interest in their own art. If any one, like Walt Whitman, penetrated to the feelings and images which the American scene was able to breed out of itself, and filled them with a frank and broad afflatus of his own, there is no doubt that he misrepresented the conscious minds of cultivated Americans; in them the head as yet did not belong to the trunk.

Nevertheless, *belles-lettres* in the United States—which after all stretch beyond New England—have always had two points of contact with the great national experiment.

One point of contact has been oratory, with that sort of poetry, patriotic, religious, or moral, which has the function of oratory. Eloquence is a republican art, as conversation is an aristocratic one. By eloquence at public meetings and dinners, in the pulpit or in the press, the impulses of the community could be brought to expression; consecrated maxims could be reapplied; the whole latent manliness and shrewdness of the nation could be mobilised. In the form of oratory reflection, rising out of the problems of action, could be turned to guide or to sanction action, and sometimes could attain, in so doing, a notable elevation of thought. Although Americans, and many other people, usually say that thought is for the sake of action, it has evidently been in these high moments, when action became incandescent in thought, that they have been most truly alive, intensively most active, and although *doing* nothing, have found at last that their existence was worth while. Reflection is itself a turn, and the top turn, given to life. Here is the second point at which literature in America has fused with the activities of the nation : it

has paused to enjoy them. Every animal
has his festive and ceremonious moments,
when he poses or plumes himself or thinks;
sometimes he even sings and flies aloft in a
sort of ecstasy.   Somewhat in the same way,
when reflection in man becomes dominant,
it may become passionate; it may create
religion or philosophy — adventures often
more thrilling than the humdrum experience they are supposed to interrupt.

This pure flame of mind is nothing new,
superadded, or alien in America.   It is
notorious how metaphysical was the passion
that drove the Puritans to those shores;
they went there in the hope of living more
perfectly in the spirit.   And their pilgrim's
progress was not finished when they had
founded their churches in the wilderness;
an endless migration of the mind was still
before them, a flight from those new idols
and servitudes which prosperity involves,
and the eternal lure of spiritual freedom
and truth.   The moral world always contains undiscovered or thinly peopled continents open to those who are more attached
to what might or should be than to what
already is.   Americans are eminently pro-

phets; they apply morals to public affairs; they are impatient and enthusiastic. Their judgements have highly speculative implications, which they often make explicit; they are men with principles, and fond of stating them. Moreover, they have an intense self-reliance; to exercise private judgement is not only a habit with them but a conscious duty. Not seldom personal conversions and mystical experiences throw their ingrained faith into novel forms, which may be very bold and radical. They are traditionally exercised about religion, and adrift on the subject more than any other people on earth; and if religion is a dreaming philosophy, and philosophy a waking religion, a people so wide awake and so religious as the old Yankees ought certainly to have been rich in philosophers.

In fact, philosophy in the good old sense of curiosity about the nature of things, with readiness to make the best of them, has not been absent from the practice of Americans or from their humorous moods; their humour and shrewdness are sly comments on the shortcomings of some polite convention that everybody accepts tacitly, yet feels to

be insecure and contrary to the principles
on which life is actually carried on. Nevertheless, with the shyness which simple competence often shows in the presence of
conventional shams, these wits have not
taken their native wisdom very seriously.
They have not had the leisure nor the
intellectual scope to think out and defend
the implications of their homely perceptions.
Their fresh insight has been whispered in
parentheses and asides; it has been humbly
banished, in alarm, from their solemn
moments. What people have respected have
been rather scraps of official philosophy, or
entire systems, which they have inherited
or imported, as they have respected operas
and art museums. To be on speaking terms
with these fine things was a part of social
respectability, like having family silver.
High thoughts must be at hand, like those
candlesticks, probably candleless, sometimes
displayed as a seemly ornament in a room
blazing with electric light. Even in William
James, spontaneous and stimulating as he
was, a certain underlying discomfort was
discernible; he had come out into the open,
into what should have been the sunshine,

but the vast shadow of the temple still stood between him and the sun. He was worried about what *ought* to be believed and the awful deprivations of disbelieving. What he called the cynical view of anything had first to be brushed aside, without stopping to consider whether it was not the true one ; and he was bent on finding new and empirical reasons for clinging to free-will, departed spirits, and tutelary gods. Nobody, except perhaps in this last decade, has tried to bridge the chasm between what he believes in daily life and the " problems " of philosophy. Nature and science have not been ignored, and " practice " in some schools has been constantly referred to ; but instead of supplying philosophy with its data they have only constituted its difficulties ; its function has been not to build on known facts but to explain them away. Hence a curious alternation and irrelevance, as between weekdays and Sabbaths, between American ways and American opinions.

That philosophy should be attached to tradition would be a great advantage, conducive to mutual understanding, to maturity, and to progress, if the tradition lay in the

highway of truth. To deviate from it in
that case would be to betray the fact that,
while one might have a lively mind, one was
not master of the subject. Unfortunately,
in the nineteenth century, in America as
elsewhere, the ruling tradition was not only
erratic and far from the highway of truth,
but the noonday of this tradition was over,
and its classic forms were outgrown. A
philosophy may have a high value, other
than its truth to things, in its truth to
method and to the genius of its author ; it
may be a feat of synthesis and imagination,
like a great poem, expressing one of the
eternal possibilities of being, although one
which the creator happened to reject when
he made this world. It is possible to be a
master in false philosophy—easier, in fact,
than to be a master in the truth, because
a false philosophy can be made as simple
and consistent as one pleases. Such had
been the masters of the tradition prevalent
in New England—Calvin, Hume, Fichte, not
to mention others more relished because less
pure ; but one of the disadvantages of such
perfection in error is that the illusion is
harder to transmit to another age and

country. If Jonathan Edwards, for instance, was a Calvinist of pristine force
and perhaps the greatest *master* in false
philosophy that America has yet produced,
he paid the price by being abandoned, even
in his lifetime, by his own sect, and seeing
the world turn a deaf ear to his logic
without so much as attempting to refute it.
One of the peculiarities of recent speculation,
especially in America, is that ideas are
abandoned in virtue of a mere change of
feeling, without any new evidence or new
arguments.  We do not nowadays refute
our predecessors, we pleasantly bid them
good-bye.  Even if all our principles are
unwittingly traditional we do not like to
bow openly to authority.  Hence masters
like Calvin, Hume, or Fichte rose before
their American admirers like formidable
ghosts, foreign and unseizable.  People re-
fused to be encumbered with any system,
even one of their own ; they were content
to imbibe more or less of the spirit of a
philosophy and to let it play on such facts
as happened to attract their attention.  The
originality even of Emerson and of William
James was of this incidental character ; they

found new approaches to old beliefs or new expedients in old dilemmas. They were not in a scholastic sense pupils of anybody or masters in anything. They hated the scholastic way of saying what they meant, if they had heard of it; they insisted on a personal freshness of style, refusing to make their thought more precise than it happened to be spontaneously; and they lisped their logic, when the logic came.

We must remember that ever since the days of Socrates, and especially after the establishment of Christianity, the dice of thought have been loaded. Certain pledges have preceded inquiry and divided the possible conclusions beforehand into the acceptable and the inacceptable, the edifying and the shocking, the noble and the base. Wonder has no longer been the root of philosophy, but sometimes impatience at having been cheated and sometimes fear of being undeceived. The marvel of existence, in which the luminous and the opaque are so romantically mingled, no longer lay like a sea open to intellectual adventure, tempting the mind to conceive some bold and curious system of the universe, on the

analogy of what had been so far discovered.
Instead, people were confronted with an orthodoxy—though not always the same orthodoxy
—*whispering mysteries and brandishing
anathemas. Their wits were absorbed in
solving traditional problems, many of them
artificial and such as the ruling orthodoxy
had created by its gratuitous assumptions.
Difficulties were therefore found in some
perfectly obvious truths; and obvious fables,
if they were hallowed by association, were
seriously weighed in the balance against one
another or against the facts; and many an
actual thing was proved to be impossible, or
was hidden under a false description. In
conservative schools the student learned and
tried to fathom the received solutions; in
liberal schools he was perhaps invited to
seek solutions of his own, but still to the
old questions. Freedom, when nominally
allowed, was a provisional freedom; if your
wanderings did not somehow bring you back
to orthodoxy you were a misguided being,
no matter how disparate from the orthodox
might be the field from which you fetched
your little harvest; and if you could not
be answered you were called superficial.

Most spirits are cowed by such disparagement ; but even those who snap their fingers at it do not escape ; they can hardly help feeling that in calling a spade a spade they are petulant and naughty ; or if their inspiration is too genuine for that, they still unwittingly shape their opinions in contrast to those that claim authority, and therefore on the same false lines—a terrible tax to pay to the errors of others ; and it is only here and there that a very great and solitary mind, like that of Spinoza, can endure obloquy without bitterness or can pass through perverse controversies without contagion.

Under such circumstances it is obvious that speculation can be frank and happy only where orthodoxy has receded, abandoning a larger and larger field to unprejudiced inquiry ; or else (as has happened among liberal Protestants) where the very heart of orthodoxy has melted, has absorbed the most alien substances, and is ready to bloom into anything that anybody finds attractive. This is the secret of that extraordinary vogue which the transcendental philosophy has had for nearly a century in Great Britain and America; it is a method which enables a man to renovate all his beliefs, scientific and religious, from the inside, giving them a new status and interpretation as phases of his own experience or imagination; so that he does not seem to himself to reject anything, and yet is bound to nothing, except to his creative self. Many too who have no inclination to practise this transcendental method—a personal, arduous, and futile art, which requires to be renewed at every moment —have been impressed with the results or the maxims of this or that transcendental philosopher, such as that every opinion leads on to another that reinterprets it, or every evil to some higher good that contains it; and they have managed to identify these views with what still seemed to them vital in religion.

In spite of this profound mutation at the core, and much paring at the edges, traditional belief in New England retained its continuity and its priestly unction; and religious teachers and philosophers could slip away from Calvinism and even from Christianity without any loss of elevation or austerity. They found it so pleasant and easy to elude the past that they really had no quarrel with it. The world, they felt, was a safe place, watched over by a kindly God, who exacted nothing but cheerfulness and good-will from his children; and the American flag was a sort of rainbow in the sky, promising that all storms were over. Or if storms came, such as the Civil War, they would not be harder to weather than was necessary to test the national spirit and raise it to a new efficiency. The subtler dangers which we may now see threatening America had not yet come in sight—material restlessness was not yet ominous, the pressure of business enterprises was not yet out of scale with the old life or out of key with the old moral harmonies. A new type of American had not appeared—the untrained, pushing, cosmopolitan orphan, cock-sure in manner but not too sure in his morality, to whom the old Yankee, with his sour integrity, is almost a foreigner. Was not " increase," in the Bible, a synonym for benefit ? Was not " abundance " the same, or almost the same, as happiness ?

Meantime the churches, a little ashamed of their past, began to court the good opinion of so excellent a world. Although called evangelical, they were far, very far, from prophesying its end, or offering a refuge from it, or preaching contempt for it ; they existed only to serve it, and their highest divine credential was that the world needed them. Irreligion, dissoluteness, and pessimism— supposed naturally to go together — could never prosper ; they were incompatible with efficiency. That was the supreme test. " Be Christians," I once heard a president of Yale College cry to his assembled pupils, " be Christians and you will be successful." Religion was indispensable and sacred, when not carried too far ; but theology might well be unnecessary. Why distract this world with talk of another ? Enough for the day was the good thereof. Religion should be disentangled as much as possible from history and authority and metaphysics, and made to rest honestly on one's fine feelings, on one's indomitable optimism and trust in life. Revelation was nothing miraculous, given once for all in some remote age and foreign country ; it must come to us directly, and with greater authority now than ever before. If evolution was to be taken seriously and to

include moral growth, the great men of the
past could only be stepping-stones to our
own dignity. To grow was to contain and
sum up all the good that had gone before,
adding an appropriate increment. Undoubtedly some early figures were beautiful,
and allowances had to be made for local
influences in Palestine, a place so much more
primitive and backward than Massachusetts.
Jesus was a prophet more winsome and nearer
to ourselves than his predecessors ; but how
could any one deny that the twenty centuries
of progress since his time must have raised
a loftier pedestal for Emerson or Channing or
Phillips Brooks ?  It might somehow not be
in good taste to put this feeling into clear
words ; one and perhaps two of these men
would have deprecated it ; nevertheless it
beamed with refulgent self-satisfaction in the
lives and maxims of most of their followers.

All this liberalism, however, never touched
the centre of traditional orthodoxy, and those
who, for all their modernness, felt that they
inherited the faith of their fathers and were
true to it were fundamentally right.  There
was still an orthodoxy among American high-
brows at the end of the nineteenth century,

dissent from which was felt to be scandalous ; it consisted in holding that the universe exists and is governed for the sake of man or of the human spirit. This persuasion, arrogant as it might seem, is at bottom an expression of impotence rather than of pride. The soul is originally vegetative ; it feels the weal and woe of what occurs within the body. With locomotion and the instinct to hunt and to flee, animals begin to notice external things also ; but the chief point noticed about them is whether they are good or bad, friendly or hostile, far or near. The station of the animal and his interests thus become the measure of all things for him, in so far as he knows them ; and this aspect of them is, by a primitive fatality, the heart of them to him. It is only reason that can discount these childish perspectives, neutralise the bias of each by collating it with the others, and masterfully conceive the field in which their common objects are deployed, discovering also the principle of foreshortening or projection which produces each perspective in turn. But reason is a later comer into this world, and weak ; against its suasion stands the mighty resistance of habit and of

C

moral presumption. It is in their interest, and to rehabilitate the warm vegetative autonomy of the primitive soul, that orthodox religion and philosophy labour in the western world—for the mind of India cannot be charged with this folly. Although inwardly these systems have not now a good conscience and do not feel very secure (for they are retrograde and sin against the light), yet outwardly they are solemn and venerable ; and they have incorporated a great deal of moral wisdom with their egotism or humanism—more than the Indians with their respect for the infinite. In deifying human interests they have naturally studied and expressed them justly, whereas those who perceive the relativity of human goods are tempted to scorn them—which is itself unreasonable—and to sacrifice them all to the single passion of worship or of despair. Hardly anybody, except possibly the Greeks at their best, has realised the sweetness and glory of being a rational animal.

The Jews, as we know, had come to think that it was the creator of the world, the God of the universe, who had taken them for his chosen people. Christians in turn had asserted that it was God in person who, having become a man, had founded their church. According to this Hebraic tradition, thè dignity of man did not lie in being a mind (which he undoubtedly is) but in being a creature materially highly favoured, with a longer life and a brighter destiny than other creatures in the world. It is remarkable how deep, in the Hebraic religions, is this interest in material existence ; so deep that we are surprised when we discover that, according to the insight of other races, this interest is the essence of irreligion. Some detachment from existence and from hopes of material splendour has indeed filtered into Christianity through Platonism. Socrates and his disciples admired this world, but they did not particularly covet it, or wish to live long in it, or expect to improve it ; what they cared for was an idea or a good which they found expressed in it, something outside it and timeless, in which the contemplative intellect might be literally absorbed. This philosophy was no less humanistic than that of the Jews, though in a less material fashion : if it did not read the universe in terms of thrift, it read it in terms of art. The pursuit

of a good, such as is presumably aimed at in
human action, was supposed to inspire every
movement in nature ; and this good, for the
sake of which the very heavens revolvèd,
was akin to the intellectual happiness of a
Greek sage. Nature was a philosopher in
pursuit of an idea. Natural science then
took a moralising turn which it has not yet
quite outgrown. Socrates required of astro-
nomy, if it was to be true science, that it
should show why *it was best* that the sun
and moon should be as they are ; and Plato,
refining on this, assures us that the eyes are
placed in the front of the head, rather than
at the back, because the front is the nobler
quarter, and that the intestines are long in
order that we may have leisure between meals
to study philosophy. Curiously enough, the
very enemies of final causes sometimes catch
this infection and attach absolute values to
facts in an opposite sense and in an inhuman
interest ; and you often hear in America
that whatever is is right. These naturalists,
while they rebuke the moralists for thinking that nature is ruled magically for our
good, think her adorable for being ruled,
in scorn of us, only by her own laws ;

and thus we oscillate between egotism and idolatry.

The Reformation did not reform this belief in the cosmic supremacy of man, or the humanity of God; on the contrary, it took it (like so much else) in terrible German earnest, not suffering it any longer to be accepted somewhat lightly as a classical figure of speech or a mystery resting on revelation. The human race, the chosen people, the Christian elect were like tabernacle within tabernacle for the spirit; but in the holy of holies was the spirit itself, one's own spirit and experience, which was the centre of everything. Protestant philosophy, exploring the domain of science and history with confidence, and sure of finding the spirit walking there, was too conscientious to misrepresent what it found. As the terrible facts could not be altered they had to be undermined. By turning psychology into metaphysics this could be accomplished, and we could reach the remarkable conclusion that the human spirit was not so much the purpose of the universe as its seat, and the only universe there was.

This conclusion, which sums up idealism

on its critical or scientific side, would not of
itself give much comfort to religious minds,
that usually crave massive support rather
than sublime independence ; it leads to the
heroic egotism of Fichte or Nietzsche rather
than to any green pastures beside any still
waters.  But the critical element in idealism
can be used to destroy belief in the natural
world ; and by so doing it can open the way
to another sort of idealism, not at all critical,
which might be called the higher superstition.  This views the world as an oracle
or charade, concealing a dramatic unity, or
formula, or maxim, which all experience
exists to illustrate.  The habit of regarding
existence as a riddle, with a surprising solution which we think we have found, should
be the source of rather mixed emotions ;
the facts remain as they were, and rival
solutions may at any time suggest themselves ; and the one we have hit on may
not, after all, be particularly comforting.
The Christian may find himself turned by it
into a heathen, the humanist into a pantheist,
and the hope with which we instinctively
faced life may be chastened into mere con-
formity.  Nevertheless, however chilling and

inhuman our higher superstition may prove, it will make us feel that we are masters of a mystical secret, that we have a faith to defend, and that, like all philosophers, we have taken a ticket in a lottery in which if we hit on the truth, even if it seems a blank, we shall have drawn the first prize.

Orthodoxy in New England, even so transformed and attenuated, did not of course hold the field alone. There are materialists by instinct in every age and country; there are always private gentlemen whom the clergy and the professors cannot deceive. Here and there a medical or scientific man, or a man of letters, will draw from his special pursuits some hint of the nature of things at large; or a political radical will nurse undying wrath against all opinions not tartly hostile to church and state. But these clever people are not organised, they are not always given to writing, nor speculative enough to make a system out of their convictions. The enthusiasts and the pedagogues naturally flock to the other camp. The very competence which scientific people and connoisseurs have in their special fields disinclines them to generalise, or renders their tradition might be making a fool of him, that prompted the hard-headed Briton, even before the Reformation, to appeal from conventional beliefs to " experience." He was anxious to clear away those sophistries and impostures of which he was particularly apprehensive, in view of the somewhat foreign character of his culture and religion. Experience, he thought, would bear unimpeachable witness to the nature of things ; for by experience he understood knowledge produced by direct contact with the object. Taken in this sense, experience is a method of discovery, an exercise of intelligence ; it is the same observation of things, strict, cumulative, and analytic, which produces the natural sciences. It rests on naturalistic assumptions (since we know when and where we find our data) and could not fail to end in materialism. What prevented British empiricism from coming to this obvious conclusion was a peculiarity of the national temperament. The Englishman is not only distrustful of too much reasoning and too much theory (and science and materialism involve a good deal of both), but he is also fond of musing and of withdrawing into his inner man. Accordingly his empiricism took an introspective form; like Hamlet he stopped at the *how*; he began to think about thinking. His first care was now to arrest experience as he underwent it; though its presence could not be denied, it came in such a questionable shape that it could not be taken at its word. This mere presence of experience, this ghostly apparition to the inner man, was all that empirical philosophy could now profess to discover. Far from being an exercise of intelligence, it retracted all understanding, all interpretation, all instinctive faith; far from furnishing a sure record of the truths of nature, it furnished a set of pathological facts, the passive subject-matter of psychology. These now seemed the only facts admissible, and psychology, for the philosophers, became the only science. Experience could discover nothing, but all discoveries had to be retracted, so that they should revert to the fact of experience and terminate there. Evidently when the naturalistic background and meaning of experience have dropped out in this way, empiricism is a form of idealism, since whatever objects we can come upon will all be *a priori* and *a fortiori* and *sensu eminentiori* ideal in the mind. The irony of logic actually made English empiricism, understood in this psychological way, the starting-point for transcendentalism and for German philosophy.

Between these two senses of the word experience, meaning sometimes contact with things and at other times absolute feeling, the empirical school in England and America has been helplessly torn, without ever showing the courage or the self-knowledge to choose between them. I think we may say that on the whole their view has been this : that feelings or ideas were absolute atoms of existence, without any ground or source, so that the elements of their universe were all mental ; but they conceived these psychical elements to be deployed in a physical time and even (since there were many simultaneous series of them) in some sort of space. These philosophers were accordingly idealists about substance but naturalists about the order and relations of existences ; and experience on their lips meant feeling when they were thinking of particulars, but when they were thinking broadly, in

matters of history or science, experience
meant the universal nebula or cataract which
these feelings composed—itself no object of
experience, but one believed in and very
imperfectly presented in imagination. These
men believed in nature, and were materialists
at heart and to all practical purposes ; but
they were shy intellectually, and seemed to
think they ran less risk of error in holding
a thing covertly than in openly professing it.

If any one, like Herbert Spencer, kept
psychology in its place and in that respect
remained a pure naturalist, he often for-
feited this advantage by enveloping the
positive information he derived from the
sciences in a whirlwind of generalisations.
The higher superstition, the notion that
nature dances to the tune of some comprehensive formula or some magic rhyme, thus
reappeared among those who claimed to
speak for natural science.  In their romantic
sympathy with nature they attributed to her
an excessive sympathy with themselves; they
overlooked her infinite complications and
continual irony, and candidly believed they
could measure her with their thumb-rules.
Why should philosophers drag a toy-net of

words, fit to catch butterflies, through the
sea of being, and expect to land all the fish
in it ? Why not take note simply of what
the particular sciences can as yet tell us of
the world ? Certainly, when put together,
they already yield a very wonderful, very
true, and very sufficient picture of it. Are
we impatient of knowing everything ? But
even if science was much enlarged it would
have limits, both in penetration and in
extent; and there would always remain, I
will not say an infinity of unsolved problems
(because " problems " are created by our
impatience or our contradictions), but an
infinity of undiscovered facts. Nature is
like a beautiful woman that may be as de-
lightfully and as truly known at a certain
distance as upon a closer view ; as to knowing her through and through, that is nonsense
in both cases, and might not reward our
pains. The love of all-inclusiveness is as
dangerous in philosophy as in art. The
savour of nature can be enjoyed by us only
through our own senses and insight, and
an outline map of the entire universe, even
if it was not fabulously concocted, would
not tell us much that was worth knowing

about the outlying parts of it. Without
suggesting for a moment that the proper
study of mankind is man only—for it may
be landscape or mathematics—we may safely
say that their proper study is what lies
within their range and is interesting to
them. For this reason the moralists who
consider principally human life and paint
nature only as a background to their figures
are apt to be better philosophers than the
speculative naturalists. In human life we are
at home, and our views on it, if one-sided,
are for that very reason expressive of our
character and fortunes. An unfortunate
peculiarity of naturalistic philosophers is
that usually they have but cursory and
wretched notions of the inner life of the
mind; they are dead to patriotism and to religion, they hate poetry and fancy and passion
and even philosophy itself; and therefore
(especially if their science too, as often
happens, is borrowed and vague) we need
not wonder if the academic and cultivated
world despises them, and harks back to the
mythology of Plato or Aristotle or Hegel,
who at least were conversant with the spirit
of man.

Philosophers are very severe towards other philosophers because they expect too much. Even under the most favourable circumstances no mortal can be asked to seize the truth in its wholeness or at its centre. As the senses open to us only partial perspectives, taken from one point of view, and report the facts in symbols which, far from being adequate to the full nature of what surrounds us, resemble the coloured signals of danger or of free way which a railway ·engine-driver peers at in the night, so our speculation, which is a sort of panoramic sense, approaches things peripherally and expresses them humanly. But how doubly dyed in this subjectivity must our thought be when an orthodoxy dominant for ages has twisted the universe into the service of moral interests, and when even the heretics are entangled in a scepticism so partial and arbitrary that it substitutes psychology, the most derivative and dubious of sciences, for the direct intelligent reading of experience! But this strain of subjectivity is not in all respects an evil; it is a warm purple dye. When a way of thinking is deeply rooted in the soil, and embodies the instincts

or even the characteristic errors of a people,
it has a value quite independent of its truth ;
it constitutes a phase of human life and
can powerfully affect the intellectual drama
in which it figures.  It is a value of this
sort that attaches to modern philosophy in
general, and very particularly to the American thinkers I am about to discuss.  There
would be a sort of irrelevance and unfair-
ness in measuring them by the standards of
pure science or even of a classic sagacity,
and reproaching them for not having reached
perfect consistency or fundamental clearness.
Men of intense feeling—and others will
hardly count—are not mirrors but lights.
If pure truth happened to be what they
passionately desired, they would seek it
single-mindedly, and in matters within their
competence they would probably find it ;
but the desire for pure truth, like any
other, must wait to be satisfied until its
organ is ripe and the conditions are favourable.  The nineteenth century was not a
time and America was not a place where such
an achievement could be expected.  There
the wisest felt themselves to be, as they
were, questioners and apostles rather than

D

# CHAPTER II

DURING some twenty-five years—fr(
1885 to 1910—there was at Harvar(
an interesting congregation of phil(
Why at Harvard in particular ?  S(
philosophy is the free pursuit of w.
arises wherever men of character a:
tration, each with his special expe1
hobby, look about them in this worl(
philosophers should be professors is
dent, and almost an anomaly.  Fr(
tion about everything is a habit to be i
but not a subject to expound ;
original system, if the philosopher :
is something dark, perilous, untest
not ripe to be taught, nor is the1
danger that any one will learn it.  T]
ine philosopher — as Royce liked
quoting the Upanishads—wanders a]

the rhinoceros. He may be followed, as he
may have been anticipated; and he may
èven be accompanied, though there is as
much danger as stimulus to him in flying
with a flock. In his disputations, if he is
drawn into them, he will still be solilo-
quising, and meeting not the arguments
persuasive to others, but only such a version
of them as his own thought can supply. The
value of his questions and answers, as Socrates
knew so well, will lie wholly in the monition
of the argument developing within him and
carrying him whithersoever it will, like a
dream or like a god. If philosophers must
earn their living and not beg (which some
of them have thought more consonant with
their vocation), it would be safer for them
to polish lenses like Spinoza, or to sit in a
black skull-cap and white beard at the door
of some unfrequented museum, selling the
catalogues and taking in the umbrellas;
these innocent ways of earning their bread-
card in the future republic would not prejudice their meditations and would keep their
eyes fixed, without undue affection, on a
characteristic bit of that real world which
it is their business to understand. Or if,

being mild and bookish, it is thought they ought to be teachers, they might teach something else than philosophy; or if philosophy is the only thing they are competent to teach, it might at least not be their own, but some classic system with which, and against which, mankind is already inoculated —preferably the civilised ethics and charming myths of Plato and Aristotle, which everybody will be the better for knowing and few the worse for believing. At best, the true philosopher can fulfil his mission very imperfectly, which is to pilot himself, or at most a few voluntary companions who may find themselves in the same boat. It is not easy for him to shout, or address a crowd; he must be silent for long seasons; for he is watching stars that move slowly and in courses that it is possible though difficult to foresee; and he is crushing all things in his heart as in a winepress, until his life and their secret flow out together.

The tendency to gather and to breed philosophers in universities does not belong to ages of free and humane reflection : it is scholastic and proper to the Middle Ages and to Germany. And the reason is not far to

seek.  When there is a philosophical orthodoxy, and speculation is expected to be a
reasoned defence of some funded inspiration,
it becomes itself corporate and traditional,
and requires centres of teaching, endowment,
and propaganda.  Fundamental questions
have been settled by the church, the government, or the Zeitgeist, and the function of
the professor, himself bred in that school, is
to transmit its lore to the next generation,
with such original touches of insight or
eloquence as he may command.  To maintain and elucidate such a tradition, all the
schools and universities of Christendom were
originally founded; and if philosophy seemed
sometimes to occupy but a small place in
them—as for instance in the old-fashioned
American college—it was only because the
entire discipline and instruction of the place
were permeated with a particular system of
faith and morals, which it was almost superfluous to teach in the abstract.  In those
universities where philosophical controversy
is rife, its traditional and scholastic character
is no less obvious ; it lives less on meditation
than on debate, and turns on proofs, objec-
tions, paradoxes, or expedients for seeming

to re-establish everything that had come to seem clearly false, by some ingenious change of front or some twist of dialectic. Its subject-matter is not so much what is known of the world, as what often very ignorant philosophers have said in answer to one another; or else, when the age is out of patience with scholasticism, orthodoxy may take refuge in intuition, and for fear of the letter without the spirit, may excuse itself from considering at all what is logical or probable, in order to embrace whatever seems most welcome and comforting. The sweet homilies of the professors then become clerical, genteel, and feminine.

Harvard College had been founded to rear puritan divines, and as Calvinism gradually dissolved, it left a void there and as it were a mould, which a philosophy expressing the same instincts in a world intellectually transformed could flow into and fill almost without knowing it. Corporate bodies are like persons, long vaguely swayed by early impressions they may have forgotten. Even when changes come over the spirit of their dream, a sense of the mission to which they were first dedicated lingers about them, and may revive, like the antiquarian and poetic Catholicism of Oxford in the nineteenth century. In academic America the Platonic and Catholic traditions had never been planted; it was only the Calvinistic tradition, when revived in some modern disguise, that could stir there the secret cord of reverence and enthusiasm. Harvard was the seminary and academy for the inner circle of Bostonians, and naturally responded to all the liberal and literary movements of which Boston was the centre. In religion it became first unitarian and afterwards neutral; in philosophy it might long have been satisfied with what other New England colleges found sufficient, namely such lofty views as the president, usually a clergyman, could introduce into his baccalaureate sermons, or into the course of lectures he might give for seniors on the evidences of Christianity or on the theory of evolution. Such philosophical initiation had sufficed for the distinguished literary men of the middle of the century, and even for so deep a sage as Emerson. But things cannot stand still, and Boston, as is well known, is not an ordinary place. When the impulse to domestic literary expression seemed to be exhausted, intellectual ambition took other forms. It was an age of science, of philology, of historical learning, and the laurels of Germany would not let Boston sleep. As it had a great public library, and hoped to have a great art museum, might it not have a great university ? Harvard in one sense was a university already, in that the college (although there was only one) was surrounded by a group of professional schools, notably those of law and medicine, in which studies requisite for the service of the community, and leading potentially to brilliant careers, were carried on with conspicuous success. The number of these professional schools might have been enlarged, as has been actually done later, until training in all the professions had been provided. But it happens that the descriptive sciences, languages, mathematics, and philosophy are not studies useful for any profession, except that of teaching these very subjects over again ; and there was no practical way of introducing them into the Harvard system except to graft them upon the curriculum of the college ; otherwise neither money nor students could

have been found for so much ornamental
learning.

This circumstance, external and irrelevant as it may seem, I think had a great
influence over the temper and quality of the
Harvard philosophers; for it mingled responsibility for the education of youth, and
much labour in it, with their pure speculation.
Teaching is a delightful paternal art, and
especially teaching intelligent and warm-
hearted youngsters, as most American collegians are; but it is an art like acting, where
the performance, often rehearsed, must be
adapted to an audience hearing it only once.
The speaker must make concessions to their
impatience, their taste, their capacity, their
prejudices, their ultimate good; he must
neither bore nor perplex nor demoralise them.
His thoughts must be such as can flow daily,
and be set down in notes; they must come
when the bell rings and stop appropriately
when the bell rings a second time. The best
that is in him, as Mephistopheles says in
*Faust*, he dare not tell them; and as the
substance of this possession is spiritual, to
withhold is often to lose it. For it is not
merely a matter of fearing not to be under-

stood, or giving offence; in the presence of
a hundred youthful upturned faces a man
cannot, without diffidence, speak in his own
person, of his own thoughts; he needs
support, in order to exert influence with a
good conscience; unless he feels that he is
the vehicle of a massive tradition, he will
become bitter, or flippant, or aggressive; if
he is to teach with good grace and modesty
and authority, it must not be he that speaks,
but science or humanity that is speaking in
him.

Now the state of Harvard College, and of
American education generally, at the time to
which I refer, had this remarkable effect on
the philosophers there : it made their sense
of social responsibility acute, because they
were consciously teaching and guiding the
community, as if they had been clergymen ; and it made no less acute their moral
loneliness, isolation, and forced self-reliance,
because they were like clergymen without a
church, and not only had no common philosophic doctrine to transmit, but were expected not to have one. They were invited
to be at once genuine philosophers and
popular professors ; and the degree to which

some of them managed to unite these con-
traries is remarkable, especially if we consider the character of the academic public
they had to serve and to please. While the
sentiments of most Americans in politics and
morals, if a little vague, are very conservative,
their democratic instincts, and the force of
circumstances, have produced a system of
education which anticipates all that the most
extreme revolution could bring about ; and
while no one dreams of forcibly suppressing
private property, religion, or the family,
American education ignores these things, and
proceeds as much as possible as if they did
not exist. The child passes very young into
a free school, established and managed by
the municipal authorities ; the teachers, even
for the older boys, are chiefly unmarried
women, sensitive, faithful, and feeble ; their
influence helps to establish that separation
which is so characteristic of America between
things intellectual, which remain wrapped in
a feminine veil and, as it were, under glass,
and the rough business and passions of life.
The lessons are ambitious in range, but are
made as easy, as interesting, and as optional
as possible ; the stress is divided between

what the child likes now and what he is going
to need in his trade or profession. The young
people are sympathetically encouraged to
instruct themselves and to educate one
another. They romp and make fun like
young monkeys, they flirt and have their
private " brain-storms " like little supermen
and superwomen. They are tremendously
in earnest about their college intrigues and
intercollegiate athletic wars. They are fond,
often compassionately fond, of their parents,
and home is all the more sacred to them in
that they are seldom there. They enjoy a
surprising independence in habits, friendships,
and opinions. Brothers and sisters often
choose different religions. The street, the
school, the young people's club, the magazine,
the popular novel, furnish their mental
pabulum. The force of example and of
passing custom is all the more irresistible in
this absence of authority and tradition ; for
this sort of independence rather diminishes
the power of being original, by supplying a
slenderer basis and a thinner soil from which
originality might spring. Uniformity is established spontaneously without discipline, as
in the popular speech and ethics of every

nation. Against this tendency to uniformity the efforts of a cultivated minority to maintain a certain distinction and infuse it into their lives and minds are not very successful. They have secondary schools for their boys in which the teachers are men, and even boarding-schools in the country, more or less Gothic in aspect and English in regimen; there are other semi-foreign institutions and circles, Catholic or Jewish, in which religion is the dominant consideration. There is also the society of the very rich, with cosmopolitan leanings and a vivacious interest in artistic undertakings and personalities. But all these distinctions, important as they may seem to those who cultivate them, are a mere shimmer and ripple on the surface of American life; and for an observer who sees things in perspective they almost disappear. By a merciful dispensation of nature, the pupils of these choice establishments, the moment they plunge into business or politics, acquire the protective colouring of their environment and become indistinguishable from the generic American. Their native disposition was after all the national one, their attempted special education was perfunctory, and the influence of their public activities and surroundings is overwhelming. American life is a powerful solvent. As it stamps the immigrant, almost before he can speak English, with an unmistakable muscular tension, cheery self-confidence and habitual challenge in the voice and eyes, so it seems to neutralise every intellectual element, however tough and alien it may be, and to fuse it in the native good-will, complacency, thoughtlessness, and optimism.

Consider, for instance, the American Catholics, of whom there are nominally many millions, and who often seem to retain their ancestral faith sincerely and affectionately. This faith took shape during the decline of the Roman empire ; it is full of large disillusions about this world and minute illusions about the other. It is ancient, metaphysical, poetic, elaborate, ascetic, autocratic, and intolerant. It confronts the boastful natural man, such as the American is, with a thousand denials and menaces. Everything in American life is at the antipodes to such a system. Yet the American Catholic is entirely at peace. His tone in everything, even in religion, is cheerfully American. It is wonderful how silently, amicably, and happily ⹂

he lives in a community whose spirit is profoundly hostile to that of his religion. He seems to take stock in his church as he might in a gold mine—sure it is a grand, dazzlïng, unique thing; and perhaps he masks, even to himself, his purely imaginative ardour about it, with the pretext that it is sure to make his fortune both in this life and in the next. His church, he will tell you, is a first-rate church to belong to; the priests are fine fellows, like the policemen; the Sisters are dear noble women, like his own sisters; his parish is flourishing, and always rebuilding its church and founding new schools, orphan asylums, sodalities, confraternities, perpetual adoration societies. No parish can raise so much money for any object, or if there are temporary troubles, the fact still remains that America has three Cardinals and that the Catholic religion is the biggest religion on earth. Attachment to his church in such a temper brings him into no serious conflict with his Protestant neighbours. They live and meet on common ground. Their respective religions pass among them for family matters, private and sacred, with no political implications.

Such was the education and such the atmosphere of intellectual innocence which prevailed in the public—mostly undergraduates —to which the Harvard philosophers adapted their teaching and to some extent their philosophy. The students were intelligent, ambitious, remarkably able to " do things " ; they were keen about the matters that had already entered into their lives, and invincibly happy in their ignorance of everything else. A gentle contempt for the past permeated their judgements. They were not accustomed to the notion of authority, nor aware that it might have legitimate grounds ; they instinctively disbelieved in the superiority of what was out of reach. About high questions of politics and religion their minds were open but vague ; they seemed not to think them of practical importance ; they acquiesced in people having any views they liked on such subjects ; the fluent and fervid enthusiasms so common among European students, prophesying about politics, philosophy, and art, were entirely unknown among them. Instead they had absorbing local traditions of their own, athletic and social, and their college life was their true education, an

E

education in friendship, co-operation, and freedom. In the eighteen-eighties a good deal of old-fashioned shabbiness and jollity lingered about Harvard. Boston and Cambridge in those days resembled in some ways the London of Dickens : the same dismal wealth, the same speechifying, the same anxious respectability, the same sordid back streets, with their air of shiftlessness and decay, the same odd figures and loud humour, and, to add a touch of horror, the monstrous suspicion that some of the inhabitants might be secretly wicked. Life, for the undergraduates, was full of droll incidents and broad farce ; it drifted good-naturedly from one commonplace thing to another. Standing packed in the tinkling horse-car, their coat-collars above their ears and their feet deep in the winter straw, they jogged in a long half-hour to Boston, there to enjoy the delights of female society, the theatre, or a good dinner. And in the summer days, for Class Day and Commencement, feminine and elderly Boston would return the visit, led by the governor of Massachusetts in his hired carriage-and-four, and by the local orators and poets, brimming with jokes and con-

ventional sentiments, and eager not so much
to speed the youngsters on their career, as
to air their own wit, and warm their hearts
with punch and with collective memories of
youth. It was an idyllic, haphazard, humor-
istic existence, without fine imagination,
without any familiar infusion of scholarship,
without articulate religion : a flutter of
intelligence in a void, flying into trivial play,
in order to drop back, as soon as college days
were over, into the drudgery of affairs.
There was the love of beauty, but without
the sight of it ; for the bits of pleasant landscape or the works of art which might break
the ugliness of the foreground were a sort of
æsthetic miscellany, enjoyed as one enjoys a
museum ; there was nothing in which the
spirit of beauty was deeply interfused, charged
with passion and discipline and intricate
familiar associations with delicate and noble
things. Of course, the sky is above every
country, and New England had brilliant sun-
sets and deep snows, and sea and woods were
at hand for the holidays ; and it was notable
how much even what a homely art or accident
might have done for the towns was studied
and admired. Old corners were pointed out

where the dingy red brick had lost its rigidity
and taken on a mossy tinge, and where here
and there a pane of glass, surviving all tenants
and housemaids, had turned violet in the
sunlight of a hundred years; and most
precious of all were the high thin elms,
spreading aloft, looped and drooping over
old streets and commons.  And yet it seemed
somehow as if the sentiment lavished on these
things had been intended by nature for something else, for something more important.
Not only had the mind of the nation been
originally somewhat chilled and impoverished
by Protestantism, by migration to a new
world, by absorption in material tasks, but
what fine sensibility lingered in an older
generation was not easily transmitted to the
young.  The young had their own ways,
which on principle were to be fostered and
respected; and one of their instincts was to
associate only with those of their own age and
calibre.  The young were simply young, and
the old simply old, as among peasants.
Teachers and pupils seemed animals of
different species, useful and well-disposed
towards each other, like a cow and a milkmaid;
periodic contributions could pass between

them, but not conversation. This circumstance shows how much American intelligence is absorbed in what is not intellectual. Their tasks and their pleasures divide people of different ages ; what can unite them is ideas, impersonal interests, liberal arts. Without these they cannot forget their mutual inferiority.

Certainly those four college years, judged by any external standard, were trivial and wasted ; but Americans, although so practical in their adult masculine undertakings, are slow to take umbrage at the elaborate playfulness of their wives and children. With the touching humility of strength, they seem to say to themselves, " Let the dear creatures have their fling, and be happy : what else are we old fellows slaving for ? " And certainly the joy of life is the crown of it ; but have American ladies and collegians achieved the joy of life ? Is that the summit ?

William James had a theory that if some scientific widower, with a child about to learn to walk, could be persuaded to allow the child's feet to be blistered, it would turn out, when the blisters were healed, that the child

would walk as well as if he had practised and
had many a fall; because the machinery
necessary for walking would have matured in
him automatically, just as the machinery for
breathing does in the womb. The case of
the old-fashioned American college may serve.
to support this theory. It blistered young
men's heads for four years and prevented
them from practising anything useful; yet
at the end they were found able to do most
things as well, or twice as well, as their con-
temporaries who had been all that time
apprenticed and chained to a desk. Man-
hood and sagacity ripen of themselves; it
suffices not to repress or distort them. The
college liberated the young man from the
pursuit of money, from hypocrisy, from the
control of women. He could grow for a time
according to his nature, and if this growth
was not guided by much superior wisdom or
deep study, it was not warped by any serious
perversion; and if the intellectual world did
not permanently entice him, are we so sure
that in philosophy, for instance, it had anything to offer that was very solid in itself,
or humanly very important? At least he
learned that such things existed, and gathered

a shrewd notion of what they could do for a man, and what they might make of him.

When Harvard was reformed—and I believe all the colleges are reformed now— the immediate object was not to refine college life or render it more scholarly, though for certain circles this was accomplished incidentally ; the object was rather to extend the scope of instruction, and make it more advanced. It is natural that every great city, the capital of any nation or region, should wish to possess a university in the literal sense of the word—an encyclopædic institute, or group of institutes, to teach and foster all the professions, all the arts, and all the sciences. Such a university need have nothing to do with education, with the transmission of a particular moral and intellectual tradition. Education might be courteously presupposed. The teacher would not be a man with his hand on a lad's shoulder, his son or young brother ; he would be an expert in some science, delivering lectures for public instruction, while perhaps privately carrying on investigations with the aid of a few disciples whom he would be training in his specialty. There would be no reason why either the professors or the auditors in such an institution should live together or should have much in common in religion, morals, or breeding, or should even speak the same language. On the contrary, if only each was competent in his way, the more miscellaneous their types the more perfect would these render their *universitas*. The public addressed, also, need not be restricted, any more than the public at a church or a theatre or a town library, by any requirements as to age, sex, race, or attainments. They would come on their own responsibility, to pursue what studies they chose, and so long as they found them profitable. Nor need there be any limit as to the subjects broached, or any division of them into faculties or departments, except perhaps for convenience in administration. One of the functions of professors would be to invent new subjects, because this world is so complex, and the play of the human mind upon it is so external and iridescent, that, as men's interests and attitude vary, fresh unities and fresh aspects are always discernible in everything.

As Harvard University developed, all

these characteristics appeared in it in a more or less marked degree; but the transformation was never complete. The centre of it remained a college, with its local constituency and rooted traditions, and its thousand or two thousand undergraduates needing to be educated. Experts in every science and money to pay them were not at hand, and the foreign talent that could be attracted did not always prove morally or socially digestible. The browsing undergraduate could simply range with a looser tether, and he was reinforced by a fringe of graduates who had not yet had enough, or who were attracted from other colleges. These graduates came to form a sort of normal school for future professors, stamped as in Germany with a Ph.D.; and the teachers in each subject became a committee charged with something of the functions of a registry office, to find places for their nurslings. The university could thus acquire a national and even an international function, drawing in distinguished talent and youthful ambition from everywhere, and sending forth in various directions its apostles of light and learning.

I think it is intelligible that in such a place and at such a crisis philosophy should have played a conspicuous part, and also that it should have had an ambiguous character. There had to be, explicit or implicit, a philosophy for the college. A place where all polite Boston has been educated for centuries cannot bely its moral principles and religious questionings; it must transmit its austere, faithful, reforming spirit. But at the same time there had now to be a philosophy for the university. A chief part of that traditional faith was the faith in freedom, in inquiry; and it was necessary, in the very interests of the traditional philosophy, to take account of all that was being said in the world, and to incorporate the spirit of the times in the spirit of the fathers. Accordingly, no single abstract opinion was particularly tabooed at Harvard; granted industry, sobriety, and some semblance of theism, no professor was expected to agree with any other. I believe the authorities would have been well pleased, for the sake of completeness, to have added a Buddhist, a Moslem, and a Catholic scholastic to the philosophical faculty, if only suitable sages could have been found, house-trained, as it were, and able to keep pace with the academic machine and .to áttract a sufficient number of pupils. But this official freedom was not true freedom, there was no happiness in it. A slight smell of brimstone lingered in the air. You might think what you liked, but you must consecrate your belief or your unbelief to the common task of encouraging everybody and helping everything on. You might almost be an atheist, if you were troubled enough about it. The atmosphere was not that of intelligence nor of science, it was that of duty.

In the academic life and methods of the university there was the same incomplete transformation. The teaching required was for the most part college teaching, in college subjects, such as might well have been entrusted to tutors; but it was given by professors in the form of lectures, excessive in number and too often repeated; and they were listened to by absent-minded youths, ill-grounded in the humanities, and not keenly alive to intellectual interests. The graduates (like the young ladies) were

more attentive and anxious not to miss
anything, but they were no better prepared
and often less intelligent; and there is no
dunce like a mature dunce. Accordingly,
the professor of philosophy had to swim
against rather a powerful current. Sometimes he succumbed to the reality; and if,
for instance, he happened to mention Darwin, and felt a blank before him, he would
add in a parenthesis, " Darwin, Charles,
author of the *Origin of Species*, 1859 ; epoch-
making work." At other times he might
lose himself altogether in the ideal and
imagine that he was publishing immortal
thoughts to the true university, to the world
at large, and was feeling an exhilarating
contact with masses of mankind, themselves
quickened by his message. He might see
in his mind's eye rows of learned men and
women before him, familiar with every
doubt, hardened to every conflict of opinion,
ready for any revolution, whose minds nothing he could say could possibly shock, or
disintegrate any further ; on the contrary,
the naked truth, which is gentle in its
austerity, might come to them as a blessed
deliverance, and he might fancy himself

for a moment a sort of hero from the realms of light descending into the nether regions and throwing a sop of reason into the jaws of snarling prejudice and frantic error. Or if the class was small, and only two or three were gathered together, he might imagine instead that he was sowing seeds of wisdom, warmed by affection, in the minds of genuine disciples, future tabernacles of the truth. It is possible that if the reality had corresponded more nearly with these dreams, and Harvard had actually been an adult university, philosophers there might have distilled their doctrines into a greater purity. As it was, Harvard philosophy had an opposite merit : it represented faithfully the complex inspiration of the place and hour. As the university was a local puritan college opening its windows to the scientific world, so at least the two most gifted of its philosophers were men of intense feeling, religious and romantic, but attentive to the facts of nature and the currents of worldly opinion; and each of them felt himself bound by two different responsibilities, that of describing things as they are, and that of finding them propitious to certain preconceived human

- desires. And while they shared this double allegiance, they differed very much in temper, education, and taste. William James was what is called an empiricist, Josiah Royce an idealist ; they were excellent friends and greatly influenced each other, and the very diversity between them rendered their conjunction typical of the state of philosophy in England and America, divided between the old British and the German schools. As if all this intellectual complication had not been enough, they were obliged to divide their energies externally, giving to their daily tasks as professors and pedagogues what duty demanded, and only the remainder to scholarship, reflection, and literary work. Even this distracting circumstance, however, had its compensations. College work was a human bond, a common practical interest ; it helped to keep up that circulation of the blood which made the whole Harvard school of philosophy a vital unit, and co-operative in its freedom. There was a general momentum in it, half institutional, half moral, a single troubled, noble, exciting life. Every one was labouring with the contradiction he felt in things, and perhaps in himself ;

all were determined to find some honest way out of it, or at least to bear it bravely. It was a fresh morning in the life of reason, cloudy but brightening.

# CHAPTER III

WILLIAM JAMES enjoyed in his youth what
are called advantages: he lived among
cultivated people, travelled, had teachers
of various nationalities. His father was
one of those somewhat obscure sages whom
early America produced: mystics of independent mind, hermits in the desert of business, and heretics in the churches. They
were intense individualists, full of venera-
tion for the free souls of their children,
and convinced that every one should paddle
his own canoe, especially on the high seas.
William James accordingly enjoyed a stimulating if slightly irregular education: he
never acquired that reposeful mastery of
particular authors and those safe ways of
feeling and judging which are fostered in
great schools and universities. In conse-

quènce he showed an almost physical horror
of club sentiment and of the stifling atmosphere of all officialdom. He had a knack-
for•drawing, and rather the temperament
of the artist; but the unlovely secrets of
nature and the troubles of man preoccupied
him, and he chose medicine for his profession.
Instead of practising, however, he turned
to teaching physiology, and from that passed
gradually to psychology and philosophy.

In his earlier years he retained some
traces of polyglot student days at Paris,
Bonn, Vienna, or Geneva; he slipped sometimes into foreign phrases, uttered in their
full vernacular; and there was an occasional
afterglow of Bohemia about him, in the
bright stripe of a shirt or the exuberance
of a tie. On points of art or medicine he
retained a professional touch and an un-
conscious ease which he hardly acquired in
metaphysics. I suspect he had heartily
admired some of his masters in those other
subjects, but had never seen a philosopher
whom he would have cared to resemble. Of
course there was nothing of the artist in
William James, as the artist is sometimes
conceived in England, nothing of the æsthete,

F

nothing affected or limp. In person he was
short rather than tall, erect, brisk, bearded,
-intensely masculine. While he shone in
expression and would have wished his style
to be noble if it could also be strong, he
preferred in the end to be spontaneous, and
to leave it at that; he tolerated slang in
himself rather than primness. The rough,
homely, picturesque phrase, whatever was
graphic and racy, recommended itself to
him ; and his conversation outdid his writing
in this respect. He believed in improvisa-
tion, even in thought; his lectures were
not minutely prepared. Know your subject
thoroughly, he used to say, and trust to
luck for the rest. There was a deep sense
of insecurity in him, a mixture of humility
with romanticism : we were likely to be
more or less wrong anyhow, but we might
be wholly sincere. One moment should
respect the insight of another, without try-
ing to establish too regimental a uniformity.
If you corrected yourself tartly, how could
you know that the correction was not the
worse mistake ? All our opinions were born
free and equal, all children of the Lord, and
if they were not consistent that was the Lord's

business, not theirs.  In reality, James was
consistent enough, as even Emerson (more
extreme in this sort of irresponsibility) was·
too: Inspiration has its limits, sometimes
very narrow ones.  But James was not
consecutive, not insistent ; he turned to a
subject afresh, without egotism or pedantry ;
he dropped his old points, sometimes very
good ones ; and he modestly looked for
light from others, who had less light than
himself.

His excursions into philosophy were accordingly in the nature of raids, and it is
easy for those who are attracted by one part
of his work to ignore other parts, in themselves perhaps more valuable.  I think that
in fact his popularity does not rest on his
best achievements.  His popularity rests on
three somewhat incidental books, *The Will
to Believe, Pragmatism,* and *The Varieties
of Religious Experience,* whereas, as it seems
to me, his best achievement is his *Principles
of Psychology.*  In this book he surveys, in
a way which for him is very systematic, a
subject made to his hand.  In its ostensible
outlook it is a treatise like any other, but
what distinguishes it is the author's gift for

evoking vividly the very life of the mind.
This is a work of imagination; and the
subject as he conceived it, which is the flux
of immediate experience in men in general,
requires imagination to read it at all. It
is a literary subject, like autobiography or
psychological fiction, and can be treated
only poetically; and in this sense Shakespeare is a better psychologist than Locke
or Kant. Yet this gift of imagination is
not merely literary; it is not useless in
divining the truths of science, and it is
invaluable in throwing off prejudice and
scientific shams. The fresh imagination and
vitality of William James led him to break
through many a false convention. He saw
that experience, as we endure it, is not a
mosaic of distinct sensations, nor the expression of separate hostile faculties, such
as reason and the passions, or sense and the
categories; it is rather a flow of mental
discourse, like a dream, in which all divisions
and units are vague and shifting, and the
whole is continually merging together and
drifting apart. It fades gradually in the
rear, like the wake of a ship, and bites into
the future, like the bow cutting the water.

For the candid psychologist, carried bodily on this voyage of discovery, the past is but a questionable report, and the future wholly indeterminate ; everything is simply what it is experienced as being.

At the same time, psychology is supposed to be a science, a claim which would tend to confine it to the natural history of man, or the study of behaviour, as is actually proposed by Auguste Comte and by some of James's own disciples, more jejune if more clear-headed than he. As matters now stand, however, psychology as a whole is not a science, but a branch of philosophy ; it brings together the literary description of mental discourse and the scientific description of material life, in order to consider the relation between them, which is the nexus of human nature.

What was James's position on this crucial question ? It is impossible to reply unequivocally. He approached philosophy as mankind originally approached it, without having a philosophy, and he lent himself to various hypotheses in various directions. He professed to begin his study on the assumptions of common sense, that there is

a material world which the animals that live
in it are able to perceive and to think about.
He gave a congruous extension to this view
in his theory that emotion is purely bodily
sensation, and also in his habit of conceiving
the mind as a total shifting sensibility. To ᶜ
pursue this path, however, would have led
him to admit that nature was automatic
and mind simply cognitive, conclusions
from which every instinct in him recoiled.
He preferred to believe that mind and
matter had independent energies and could
lend one another a hand, matter operating
by motion and mind by intention. This
dramatic, amphibious way of picturing causation is natural to common sense, and might
be defended if it were clearly defined ; but
James was insensibly carried away from it
by a subtle implication of his method. This
implication was that experience or mental
discourse not only constituted a set of
substantive facts, but the *only* substantive
facts ; all else, even that material world
which his psychology had postulated, could
be nothing but a verbal or fantastic symbol
for sensations in their experienced order.
So that while nominally the door was kept

open to any hypothesis regarding the conditions of the psychological flux, in truth the question was prejudged. The hypotheses, which were parts of this psychological flux, could have no object save other parts of it. That flux itself, therefore, which he could picture so vividly, was the fundamental existence. The *sense* of bounding over the waves, the *sense* of being on an adventurous voyage, was the living fact; the rest was dead reckoning. Where one's gift is, there will one's faith be also; and to this poet appearance was the only reality.

This sentiment, which always lay at the back of his mind, reached something like formal expression in his latest writings, where he sketched what he called radical empiricism. The word experience is like a shrapnel shell, and bursts into a thousand meanings. Here we must no longer think of its setting, its discoveries, or its march; to treat it radically we must abstract its immediate objects and reduce it to pure data. It is obvious (and the sequel has already proved) that experience so understood would lose its romantic signification, as a personal adventure or a response to the shocks of fortune. " Experi-

ence " would turn into a cosmic dance of absolute entities created and destroyed *in vacuo*
according to universal laws, or perhaps by
chance. No minds would gather this experience, and no material agencies would impose
it; but the immediate objects present to
any one would simply be parts of the universal
fireworks, continuous with the rest, and all the
parts, even if not present to anybody, would
have the same status. Experience would
then not at all resemble what Shakespeare
reports or what James himself had described
in his psychology. If it could be experienced
as it flows in its entirety (which is fortunately
impracticable), it would be a perpetual mathematical nightmare. Every whirling atom,
every changing relation, and every incidental
perspective would be a part of it. I am far
from wishing to deny for a moment the
scientific value of such a cosmic system, if it
can be worked out ; physics and mathematics
seem to me to plunge far deeper than literary
psychology into the groundwork of this
world ; but human experience is the stuff of
literary psychology; we cannot reach the stuff
of physics and mathematics except by arrest-
ing or even hypostatising some elements of

appearance, and expanding them on an abstracted and hypothetical plane of their own. Experience, as memory and literature rehearse it, remains nearer to us than that : it is something dreamful, passionate, dramatic, and significative.

Certainly this personal human experience, expressible in literature and in talk, and no cosmic system however profound, was what James knew best and trusted most. Had he seen the developments of his radical empiricism, I cannot help thinking he would have marvelled that such logical mechanisms should have been hatched out of that egg. The principal problems and aspirations that haunted him all his life long would lose their meaning in that cosmic atmosphere. The pragmatic nature of truth, for instance, would never suggest itself in the presence of pure data ; but a romantic mind soaked in agnosticism, conscious of its own habits and assuming an environment the exact structure of which can never be observed, may well convince itself that, for experience, truth is nothing but a happy use of signs— which is indeed the truth of literature. But if we once accept *any* system of the universe as literally true, the value of convenient signs to prepare us for such experience as is yet absent cannot be called truth : it is plainly nothing but a necessary inaccuracy. So, too, with the question of the survival of the human individual after death. For radical empiricism a human individual is simply a certain cycle or complex of terms, like any other natural fact ; that some echoes of his mind should recur after the regular chimes have ceased, would have nothing paradoxical about it. A mathematical world is a good deal like music, with its repetitions and trans-positions, and a little trill, which you might call a person, might well peep up here and there all over a vast composition. Some-thing of that sort may be the truth of spiritualism ; but it is not what the spirit-ualists imagine. Their whole interest lies not in the experiences they have, but in the interpretation they give to them, assigning them to troubled spirits in another world ; but both another world and a spirit are notions repugnant to a radical empiricism.

I think it is important to remember, if we are not to misunderstand William James, that his radical empiricism and pragmatism were

in his own mind only methods ; his doctrine,
if he may be said to have had one, was
agnosticism. And just because he was an
agnostic (feeling instinctively that beliefs and
opinions, if they had any objective beyond
themselves, could never be sure they had
attained it), he seemed in one sense so favourable to credulity. He was not credulous
himself, far from it ; he was well aware that
the trust he put in people or ideas might
betray him. For that very reason he was
respectful and pitiful to the trustfulness of
others. Doubtless they were wrong, but
who were we to say so ? In his own person
he was ready enough to face the mystery of
things, and whatever the womb of time might
bring forth ; but until the curtain was rung
down on the last act of the drama (and it
might have no last act !) he wished the intellectual cripples and the moral hunchbacks not
to be jeered at ; perhaps they might turn
out to be the heroes of the play. Who could
tell what heavenly influences might not pierce
to these sensitive half-flayed creatures, which
are lost on the thick-skinned, the sane, and
the duly goggled ? We must not suppose,
however, that James meant these contrite

and romantic suggestions dogmatically. The agnostic, as well as the physician and neurologist in him, was never quite eclipsed. The hope that some new revelation might come from the lowly and weak could never mean to him what it meant to the early Christians. For him it was only a right conceded to them to experiment with their special faiths ; he did not expect such faiths to be discoveries of absolute fact, which everybody else might be constrained to recognise. If any one had made such a claim, and had seemed to have some chance of imposing it universally, James would have been the first to turn against him ; not, of course, on the ground that it was *impossible* that such an orthodoxy should be true, but with a profound conviction that it was to be feared and distrusted. No : the degree of authority and honour to be accorded to various human faiths was a moral question, not a theoretical one. All faiths were what they were experienced as being, in their capacity of faiths ; these faiths, not their objects, were the hard facts we must respect. We cannot pass, except under the illusion of the moment, to anything firmer. or on a deeper level. There was accordingly no sense of security, no joy, in James's apology for personal religion. He did not really believe ; he merely believed in the right of believing that you might be right if you believed.

It is this underlying agnosticism that explains an incoherence which we might find in his popular works, where the story and the moral do not seem to hang together. Professedly they are works of psychological observation ; but the tendency and suasion in them seems to run to disintegrating the idea of truth, recommending belief without reason, and encouraging superstition. A psychologist who was not an agnostic would have indicated, as far as possible, whether the beliefs and experiences he was describing were instances of delusion or of rare and fine perception, or in what measure they were a mixture of both. But James—and this is what gives such romantic warmth to these writings of his—disclaims all antecedent or superior knowledge, listens to the testimony of each witness in turn, and only by accident allows us to feel that he is swayed by the eloquence and vehemence of some of them rather than of others. This method is modest,

generous, and impartial; but if James intended, as I think he did, to picture the
*drama* of human belief, with its risks and
triumphs, the method was inadequate.
Dramatists never hesitate to assume, and
to let the audience perceive, who is good and
who bad, who wise and who foolish, in their
pieces ; otherwise their work would be as
impotent dramatically as scientifically. The
tragedy and comedy of life lie precisely in the
contrast between the illusions or passions of
the characters and their true condition and
fate, hidden from them at first, but evident
to the author and the public. If in our
diffidence and scrupulous fairness we refuse
to take this judicial attitude, we shall be led
to strange conclusions. The navigator, for
instance, trusting his "experience" (which
here, as in the case of religious people, means
his imagination and his art), insists on believing that the earth is spherical; he has sailed
round it. That is to say, he has seemed to
himself to steer westward and westward, and
has seemed to get home again. But how
should he know that home is now where it
was before, or that his past and present
impressions of it come from the same, or

from any, material object ? How should he
know that space is as trim and tri-dimen-
sional as the discredited Euclidians used to
say it was ? If, on the contrary, my worthy
aunt, trusting to her longer and less ambiguous experience of her garden, insists that
the earth is flat, and observes that the theory
that it is round, which is only a theory, is
much less often tested and found useful than
her own perception of its flatness, and that
moreover that theory is pedantic, intellectual-
istic, and a product of academies, and a rash
dogma to impose on mankind for ever and
ever, it might seem that on James's principle
we ought to agree with her. But no ; on
James's real principles we need not agree
with her, nor with the navigator either.
Radical empiricism, which is radical agnosticism, delivers us from so benighted a choice.
For the quarrel becomes unmeaning when we
remember that the earth is *both* flat and
round, if it is experienced as being both.
The substantive fact is not a single object
on which both the perception and the theory
are expected to converge ; the substantive
facts are the theory and the perception themselves. And we may note in passing that

empiricism, when it ceases to value experience as a means of discovering external things, can give up its ancient prejudice in favour of sense as against imagination, for imagination and thought are immediate experiences as much as sensation is : they are therefore, for absolute empiricism, no less actual ingredients of reality.

In *The Varieties of Religious Experience* we find the same apologetic intention running through a vivid account of what seems for the most part (as James acknowledged) religious disease. Normal religious experience is hardly described in it. Religious experience, for the great mass of mankind, consists in simple faith in the truth and benefit of their religious traditions. But to James something so conventional and rationalistic seemed hardly experience and hardly religious ; he was thinking only of irruptive visions and feelings as interpreted by the mystics who had them. These interpretations he ostensibly presents, with more or less wistful sympathy, for what they were worth ; but emotionally he wished to champion them. The religions that had sprung up in America spontaneously — communistic, hysterical, spiritistic, or medicinal—were despised by select and superior people. You might inquire into them, as you might go slum-ming, but they remained suspect and distasteful. This picking up of genteel skirts on the part of his acquaintance prompted William James to roll up his sleeves—not for a knock-out blow, but for a thorough clinical demonstration. He would tenderly vivisect the experiences in question, to show how living they were, though of course he could not guarantee, more than other surgeons do, that the patient would survive the operation. An operation that eventually kills may be technically successful, and the man may die cured ; and so a description of religion that showed it to be madness might first show how real and how warm it was, so that if it perished, at least it would perish understood.

I never observed in William James any personal anxiety or enthusiasm for any of these dubious tenets. His conception even of such a thing as free-will, which he always ardently defended, remained vague ; he avoided defining even what he conceived to be desirable in such matters. But he wished to protect the weak against the strong, and what he hated beyond everything was the *non possumus* of any constituted authority. Philosophy for him had a Polish constitution ; so long as a single vote was cast against the majority, nothing could pass. The suspense of judgement which he had imposed on himself as a duty, became almost a necessity. I think it would have depressed him if he had had to confess that any important question was finally settled. He would still have hoped that something might turn up on the other side, and that just as the scientific hangman was about to despatch the poor convicted prisoner, an unexpected witness would ride up in hot haste, and prove him innocent. Experience seems to most of us to lead to conclusions, but empiricism has sworn never to draw them.

In the discourse on " The Energies of Men," certain physiological marvels are recorded, as if to suggest that the resources of our minds and bodies are infinite, or can be infinitely enlarged by divine grace. Yet James would not, I am sure, have accepted that inference. He would, under pressure, have drawn in his mystical horns under his scientific shell; but he was not naturalist enough to feel instinctively that the wonderful and the natural are all of a piece, and that only our degree of habituation distinguishes them. A nucleus, which we may poetically call the soul, certainly lies within us, by which our bodies and minds are generated and controlled, like an army by a government. In this nucleus, since nature in a small compass has room for anything, vast quantities of energy may well be stored up, which may be tapped on occasion, or which may serve like an electric spark to let loose energy previously existing in the grosser parts. But the absolute autocracy of this central power, or its success in imposing extraordinary trials on its subjects, is not an obvious good. Perhaps, like a democratic government, the soul is at its best when it merely collects and co-ordinates the impulses coming from the senses. The inner man is at times a tyrant, parasitical, wasteful, and voluptuous. At other times he is fanatical and mad. When he asks for and obtains violent exertions from the body, the question often is, as with the exploits of conquerors and conjurers, whether the impulse to do such prodigious things was

not gratuitous, and the things nugatory.
Who would wish to be a mystic ?  James
himself, who by nature was a spirited rather
than a spiritual man, had no liking for sancti-
monious transcendentalists, visionaries, or
ascetics; he hated minds that run thin.  But
he hastened to correct this manly impulse,
lest it should be unjust, and forced himself to
overcome his repugnance.  This was made
easier when the unearthly phenomenon had
a healing or saving function in the everyday
material world ;  miracle then re-established
its ancient identity with medicine, and both
of them were humanised.  Even when this
union was not attained, James was reconciled
to the miracle-workers partly by his great
charity, and partly by his hunter's instinct
to follow a scent, for he believed discoveries
to be imminent.  Besides, a philosopher who is
a teacher of youth is more concerned to give
people a right start than a right conclusion.
James fell in with the hortatory tradition of
college sages ;  he turned his psychology,
whenever he could do so honestly, to purposes
of edification ;  and his little sermons on
habit, on will, on faith, and this on the latent
capacities of men, were fine and stirring, and

just the sermons to preach to the young
Christian soldier.  He was much less sceptical
in morals than in science.  He seems to have
felt sure that certain thoughts and hopes—
those familiar to a liberal Protestantism—
were every man's true friends in life.  This
assumption would have been hard to defend
if he or those he habitually addressed had
ever questioned it ; yet his whole argument
for voluntarily cultivating these beliefs rests
on this assumption, that they are beneficent.
Since, whether we will or no, we cannot escape
the risk of error, and must succumb to some
human or pathological bias, at least we might
do so gracefully and in the form that would
profit us most, by clinging to those prejudices
which help us to lead what we all feel is a
good life.  But what is a good life ?  Had
William James, had the people about him,
had modern philosophers anywhere, any
notion of that ?  I cannot think so.  They
had much experience of personal goodness,
and love of it ; they had standards of
character and right conduct ; but as to what
might render human existence good, excellent,
beautiful, happy, and worth having as a
whole, their notions were utterly thin and

barbarous.  They had forgotten the Greeks,
or never known them.

 This argument accordingly suffers from
the same weakness as the similar argument
of Pascal in favour of Catholic orthodoxy.
You should force yourself to believe in it,
he said, because if you do so and are right
you win heaven, while if you are wrong
you lose nothing.  What would Protestants,
Mohammedans, and Hindus say to that ?
Those alternatives of Pascal's are not the
sole nor the true alternatives ; such a wager
—betting on the improbable because you
are offered big odds—is an unworthy parody
of the real choice between wisdom and folly.
There is no heaven to be won in such a
spirit, and if there was, a philosopher would
despise it.  So William James would have us
bet on immortality, or bet on our power to
succeed, because if we win the wager we can
live to congratulate ourselves on our true
instinct, while we lose nothing if we have
made a mistake ; for unless you have the
satisfaction of finding that you have been
right, the dignity of having been right is
apparently nothing.  Or if the argument
is rather that these beliefs, whether true or

false, make life better in this world, the thing is simply false. To be boosted by an illusion is not to live better than to live in harmony with the truth; it is not nearly so safe, not nearly so sweet, and not nearly so fruitful. These refusals to part with a decayed illusion are really an infection to the mind. Believe, certainly; we cannot help believing; but believe rationally, holding what seems certain for certain, what seems probable for probable, what seems desirable for desirable, and what seems false for false.

In this matter, as usual, James had a true psychological fact and a generous instinct behind his confused moral suggestions. It is a psychological fact that men are influenced in their beliefs by their will and desires; indeed, I think we can go further and say that in its essence belief is an expression of impulse, of readiness to act. It is only peripherally, as our action is gradually adjusted to things, and our impulses to our possible or necessary action, that our ideas begin to hug the facts, and to acquire a true, if still a symbolic, significance. We do not need a will to believe; we only need a will to study the object in which we are

inevitably believing. But James was thinking less of belief in what we find than of
belief in what we hope for : a belief which is
not at all clear and not at all necessary in the
life of mortals. Like most Americans, however, only more lyrically, James felt the call
of the future and the assurance that it
could be made far better, totally other,
than the past. The pictures that religion
had painted of heaven or the millennium
were not what he prized, although his
Swedenborgian connection might have made
him tender to them, as perhaps it did to
familiar spirits. It was the moral succour
offered by religion, its open spaces, the
possibility of miracles *in extremis*, that must
be retained. If we recoiled at the thought of
being dupes (which is perhaps what nature
intended us to be), were we less likely to be
dupes in disbelieving these sustaining truths
than in believing them ? Faith was needed
to bring about the reform of faith itself, as
well as all other reforms.

In some cases faith in success could nerve
us to bring success about, and so justify
itself by its own operation. This is a thought
typical of James at his worst—a worst in

which there is always a good side. Here
again psychological observation is used with
the best intentions to hearten oneself and
other people; but the fact observed is not
at all understood, and a moral twist is given
to it which (besides being morally questionable) almost amounts to falsifying the fact
itself. Why does belief that you can jump a
ditch help you to jump it ? Because it is a
symptom of the fact that you *could* jump
it, that your legs were fit and that the
ditch was two yards wide and not twenty.
A rapid and just appreciation of these facts
has given you your confidence, or at least has
made it reasonable, manly, and prophetic;
otherwise you would have been a fool and
got a ducking for it. Assurance is con-
temptible and fatal unless it is self-knowledge. If you had been rattled you might
have failed, because that would have been
a symptom of the fact that you were out of
gear; you would have been afraid because
you trembled, as James at his best pro-
claimed. You would never have quailed if
your system had been reacting smoothly to
its opportunities, any more than you would
totter and see double if you were not intoxi-

cated. Fear is a sensation of actual nerv-
ousness and disarray, and confidence a
sensation of actual readiness; they are not
disembodied feelings, existing for no reason,
the devil Funk and the angel Courage, one
or the other of whom may come down
arbitrarily into your body, and revolution-
ise it. That is childish mythology, which
survives innocently enough as a figure of
speech, until a philosopher is found to take
that figure of speech seriously. Nor is the
moral suggestion here less unsound. What
is good is not the presumption of power,
but the possession of it: a clear head, aware
of its resources, not a fuddled optimism, calling up spirits from the vasty deep. Courage
is not a virtue, said Socrates, unless it is also
wisdom. Could anything be truer both of
courage in doing and of courage in believing?
But it takes tenacity, it takes *reasonable*
courage, to stick to scientific insights such
as this of Socrates or that of James about the
emotions; it is easier to lapse into the traditional manner, to search natural philosophy
for miracles and moral lessons, and in morals
proper, in the reasoned expression of preference, to splash about without a philosophy.

William James shared the passions of liberalism. He belonged to the left, which, as they say in Spain, is the side of the heart, as the right is that of the liver; at any rate there was much blood and no gall in his philosophy. He was one of those elder Americans still disquieted by the ghost of tyranny, social and ecclesiastical. Even the beauties of the past troubled him; he had a puritan feeling that they were tainted. They had been cruel and frivolous, and must have suppressed far better things. But what, we may ask, might these better things be? It may do for a revolutionary politician to say: " I may not know what I want— except office—but I know what I don't want "; it will never do for a philosopher. Aversions and fears imply principles of preference, goods acknowledged; and it is the philosopher's business to make these goods explicit. Liberty is not an art, liberty must be used to bring some natural art to fruition. Shall it be simply eating and drinking and wondering what will happen next? If there is some deep and settled need in the heart of man, to give direction to his efforts, what else should a philosopher do but discover and announce what that need is ?

· There is a sense in which James was not a philosopher at all.  He once said to me : " What a curse philosophy would be if we couldn't forget all about it ! " In other words, philosophy was not to him what it has been to so many, a consolation and sanctuary in a life which would have been unsatisfying without it.  It would be incongruous, therefore, to expect of him that he should build a philosophy like an edifice to go and live in for good.  Philosophy to him was rather like a maze in which he happened to find himself wandering, and what he was looking for was the way out.  In the presence of theories of any sort he was attentive, puzzled, suspicious, with a certain inner prompting to disregard them.  He lived all his life among them, as a child lives among grown-up people; what a relief to turn from those stolid giants, with their prohibitions and exactions and tiresome talk, to another real child or a nice animal !  Of course grown-up people are useful, and so James considered that theories might be ; but in themselves, to live with, they were rather in the way, and at bottom our natural enemies. It was well to challenge one or another of them when you got a chance; perhaps that challenge might break some spell, transform the strange landscape, and simplify life. A theory while you were creating or using it was like a story you were telling yourself or a game you were playing; it was a warm, self-justifying thing then; but when the glow of creation or expectation was over, a theory was a phantom, like a ghost, or like the minds of other people. To all other people, even to ghosts, William James was the soul of courtesy; and he was civil to most theories as well, as to more or less interesting strangers that invaded him. Nobody ever recognised more heartily the chance that others had of being right, and the right they had to be different. Yet when it came to understanding what they meant, whether they were theories or persons, his intuition outran his patience; he made some brilliant impressionistic sketch in his fancy and called it by their name. This sketch was as often flattered as distorted, and he was at times the dupe of his desire to be appreciative and

give the devil his due ; he was too impulsive
for exact sympathy ; too subjective, too
romantic, to be just.  Love is very penetrating, but it penetrates to possibilities
rather than to facts.  The logic of opinions,
as well as the exact opinions themselves,
were not things James saw easily, or traced
with pleasure.  He liked to take things one
by one, rather than to put two and two
together.  He was a mystic, a mystic in
love with life.  He was comparable to Rous-
seau and to Walt Whitman ; he expressed a
generous and tender sensibility, rebelling
against sophistication, and preferring daily
sights and sounds, and a vague but indomitable faith in fortune, to any settled intellectual
tradition calling itself science or philosophy.

A prophet is not without honour save in
his own country ;  and until the return wave
of James's reputation reached America from
Europe, his pupils and friends were hardly
aware that he was such a distinguished man.
Everybody liked him, and delighted in him
for his generous, gullible nature and brilliant
sallies.  He was a sort of Irishman among
the Brahmins, and seemed hardly imposing
enough for a great man.  They laughed at

his erratic views and his undisguised limita-
tions. Of course a conscientious professor
ought to know everything he professes to
know, but then, they thought, a dignified professor ought to seem to know everything. The
precise theologians and panoplied idealists,
who exist even in America, shook their heads.
What sound philosophy, said they to themselves, could be expected from an irresponsible
doctor, who was not even a college graduate,
a crude empiricist, and vivisector of frogs ?
On the other hand, the solid men of business
were not entirely reassured concerning a
teacher of youth who seemed to have no
system in particular—the ignorant rather
demand that the learned should have a
system in store, to be applied at a pinch;
and they could not quite swallow a private
gentleman who dabbled in hypnotism, fre-
quented mediums, didn't talk like a book,
and didn't write like a book, except like
one of his own. Even his pupils, attached
as they invariably were to his person, felt
some doubts about the profundity of one
who was so very natural, and who after some
interruption during a lecture—and he said
life was a series of interruptions—would slap

his forehead and ask the man in the front row " What *was* I talking about ? " Perhaps in the first years of his teaching he felt a little in the professor's chair as a military man might feel when obliged to read the prayers at a funeral. He probably conceived what he said more deeply than a more scholastic mind might have conceived it ; yet he would have been more comfortable if some one else had said it for him. He liked to open the window, and look out for a moment. I think he was glad when the bell rang, and he could be himself again until the next day. But in the midst of this routine of the class-room the spirit would sometimes come upon him, and, leaning his head on his hand, he would let fall golden words, picturesque, fresh from the heart, full of the knowledge of good and evil. Incidentally there would crop up some humorous characterisation, some candid confession of doubt or of instinctive preference, some pungent scrap of learning ; radicalisms plunging sometimes into the sub-soil of all human philosophies ; and, on occasion, thoughts of simple wisdom and wistful piety, the most unfeigned and manly that anybody ever had.

# CHAPTER IV

## JOSIAH ROYCE

MEANTIME the mantle of philosophical authority had fallen at Harvard upon other shoulders. A young Californian, Josiah Royce, had come back from Germany with a reputation for wisdom; and even without knowing that he had already produced a new proof of the existence of God, merely to look at him you would have felt that he was a philosopher; his great head seemed too heavy for his small body, and his portentous brow, crowned with thick red hair, seemed to crush the lower part of his face. " Royce," said William James of him, " has an indecent exposure of forehead." There was a suggestion about him of the benevolent ogre or the old child, in whom a preternatural sharpness of insight lurked beneath a grotesque mask. If you gave him any cue, or

even without one, he could discourse broadly
on any subject; you never caught him napping.
Whatever the text-books and encyclopædias
could tell him, he knew; and if the impres-
sion he left on your mind was vague, that
was partly because, in spite of his compre-
hensiveness, he seemed to view everything
in relation to something else that remained
untold.  His approach to anything was
oblique; he began a long way off, perhaps
with the American preface of a funny story;
and when the point came in sight, it was at
once enveloped again in a cloud of qualifica-
tions, in the parliamentary jargon of philosophy.  The tap once turned on, out flowed
the stream of systematic disquisition, one
hour, two hours, three hours of it, according
to demand or opportunity.  The voice, too,
was merciless and harsh.  You felt the
overworked, standardised, academic engine,
creaking and thumping on at the call of duty
or of habit, with no thought of sparing itself
or any one else.  Yet a sprightlier soul
behind this performing soul seemed to watch
and laugh at the process.  Sometimes a
merry light would twinkle in the little eyes,
and a bashful smile would creep over the

uncompromising mouth. A sense of the paradox, the irony, the inconclusiveness of the whole argument would pierce to the surface, like a white-cap bursting here and there on the heavy swell of the sea.

His procedure was first to gather and digest whatever the sciences or the devil might have to say. He had an evident sly pleasure in the degustation and savour of difficulties; biblical criticism, the struggle for life, the latest German theory of sexual insanity, had no terrors for him; it was all grist for the mill, and woe to any tender thing, any beauty or any illusion, that should get between that upper and that nether millstone! He seemed to say: If I were not Alexander how gladly would I be Diogenes, and if I had not a system to defend, how easily I might tell you the truth. But after the sceptic had ambled quizzically over the ground, the prophet would mount the pulpit to survey it. He would then prove that in spite of all those horrors and contradictions, or rather because of them, the universe was absolutely perfect. For behind that mocking soul in him there was yet another, a devout and

heroic soul. Royce was heir to the Calvinistic tradition ; piety, to his mind, consisted
in trusting divine providence and justice,
while emphasising the most terrifying truths
about one's own depravity and the sinister
holiness of God. He accordingly addressed
himself, in his chief writings, to showing
that all lives were parts of a single divine
life in which all problems were solved and
all evils justified.

It is characteristic of Royce that in his
proof of something sublime, like the existence
of God, his premiss should be something sad
and troublesome, the existence of error.
Error exists, he tells us, and common sense
will readily agree, although the fact is not
unquestionable, and pure mystics and pure
sensualists deny it. But if error exists,
Royce continues, there must be a truth
from which it differs ; and the existence of
truth (according to the principle of idealism,
that nothing can exist except for a mind
that knows it) implies that some one knows
the truth ; but as to know the truth
thoroughly, and supply the corrective to
every possible error, involves omniscience,
we have proved the existence of an omniscient

mind or universal thought; and this is
almost, if not quite, equivalent to the
existence of God.                          •

What carried Royce over the evident
chasms and assumptions in this argument
was his earnestness and passionate eloquence.
He passed for an eminent logician, because he
was dialectical and fearless in argument and
delighted in the play of formal relations ; he
was devoted to chess, music, and mathematics ; but all this show of logic was but a
screen for his heart, and in his heart there was
no clearness. His reasoning was not pure
logic or pure observation ; it was always
secretly enthusiastic or malicious, and the
result it arrived at had been presupposed.
Here, for instance, no unprejudiced thinker,
not to speak of a pure logician, would have
dreamt of using the existence of error to
found the being of truth upon. Error is a
biological accident which may any day cease
to exist, say at the extinction of the human
race ; whereas the being of truth or fact is
involved indefeasibly and eternally in the
existence of anything whatever, past, present,
or future ; every event of itself renders true
or false any proposition that refers to it. No

one would conceive of such a thing as error or suspect its presence, unless he had already found or assumed many a truth; nor could anything be an error actually unless the truth was definite and real. All this Royce of course recognised, and it was in some sense the heart of what he meant to assert and to prove; but it does not need proving and hardly asserting. What needed proof was something else, of less logical importance but far greater romantic interest, namely, that the truth was hovering over us and about to descend into our hearts; and this Royce was not disinclined to confuse with the being of truth, so as to bring it within the range of logical argument. He was tormented by the suspicion that he might be himself in the toils of error, and fervently aspired to escape from it. Error to him was no natural, and in itself harmless, incident of finitude; it was a sort of sin, as finitude was too. It was a part of the problem of evil; a terrible and urgent problem when your first postulate or dogma is that moral distinctions and moral experience are the substance of the world, and not merely an incident in it. The mere being of truth, which is all a logician needs,

# ``

would not help him in this wrestling for
personal salvation; as he keenly felt and
often said, the truth is like the stars, always
laughing at us. Nothing would help him but
*possession* of the truth, something eventual
and terribly problematic. He longed to
believe that all his troubles and questions,
some day and somewhere, must find their
solution and quietus; if not in his own mind,
in some kindred spirit that he could, to that
extent, identify with himself. There must
be not only cold truth, not even cold truth
personified, but victorious *knowledge* of the
truth, breaking like a sun-burst through the
clouds of error. The nerve of his argument
was not logical at all; it was a confession of
religious experience, in which the agonised
consciousness of error led to a strong imaginative conviction that the truth would be found
at last.

The truth, as here conceived, meant the
whole truth about everything; and certainly,
if any plausible evidence for such a conclusion
could be adduced, it would be interesting to
learn that we are destined to become omniscient, or are secretly omniscient already.
Nevertheless, the aspiration of all religious

minds does not run that way.   Aristotle tells
us that there are many things it is better not
to know;   and his sublime deity is happily
ignorant of our errors and of our very existence; more emphatically so the even sublimer
deities of Plotinus and the Indians.   The
omniscience which our religion attributes to
God as the searcher of hearts and the judge
of conduct has a moral function rather than
a logical one; it prevents us from hiding our
sins or being unrecognised in our merits; it
is not conceived to be requisite in order that
it may be true that those sins or merits have
existed.   Atheists admit the facts, but they
are content or perhaps relieved that they
should pass unobserved.   But here again
Royce slipped into a romantic equivocation
which a strict logician would not have
tolerated.   Knowledge of the truth, a passing
psychological possession, was substituted for
the truth known, and this at the cost of rather
serious ultimate confusions.   It is the truth
itself, the facts in their actual relations, that
honest opinion appeals to, not to another
opinion or instance of knowledge; and if, in
your dream of warm sympathy and public
corroboration, you lay up your treasure in

some instance of knowledge, which time and
doubt might corrupt, you have not laid up
your treasure in heaven.  In striving to prove
the being of truth, the young Royce absurdly
treated it as doubtful, setting a bad example
to the pragmatists ;  while in striving to lend
a psychological quality to this truth and
turning it into a problematical instance of
knowledge, he unwittingly deprived it of all
authority and sublimity.  To personify the
truth is to care less for truth than for the corroboration and sympathy which the truth,
become human, might bring to our opinions.
It is to set up another thinker, ourself enlarged, to vindicate us ;  without considering
that this second thinker would be shut up,
like us, in his own opinions, and would need
to look to the truth beyond him as much as
we do.

To the old problem of evil Royce could
only give an old answer, although he redis-
covered and repeated it for himself in many
ways, since it was the core of his whole
system.  Good, he said, is essentially the
struggle with evil and the victory over it ;
so that if evil did not exist, good would be
impossible.  I do not think this answer set

him at rest ; he could hardly help feeling that
all goods are not of that bellicose description,
and that not all evils produce a healthy re-
action or are swallowed up in victory ; yet
the fact that the most specious solution to
this problem of evil left it unsolved was in its
way appropriate ; for if the problem had
been really solved, the struggle to find a
solution and the faith that there was one
would come to an end ; yet perhaps this faith
and this struggle are themselves the supreme
good.  Accordingly the true solution of this
problem, which we may all accept, is that no
solution can ever be found.

Here is an example of the difference
between the being of truth and the ultimate
solution of all our problems.  There is
certainly a truth about evil, and in this case
not an unknown truth ; yet it is no solution
to the " problem " which laid the indomitable
Royce on the rack.  If a younger son asks
why he was not born before his elder brother,
that question may represent an intelligible
state of his feelings ; but there is no answer
to it, because it is a childish question.  So
the question why it is right that there should
be any evil is itself perverse and raised by

false presumptions. To an unsophisticated
mortal the existence of evil presents a task,
never a problem. Evil, like error, is an
incident of animal life, inevitable in a crowded
and unsettled world, where one spontaneous
movement is likely to thwart another, and
all to run up against material impossibilities.
While life lasts this task is recurrent, and
every creature, in proportion to the vitality
and integrity of his nature, strives to remove
or abate those evils of which he is sensible.
When the case is urgent and he is helpless,
he will cry out for divine aid ; and (if he does
not perish first) he will soon see this aid
coming to him through some shift in the
circumstances that renders his situation en-
durable. Positive religion takes a naturalistic view of things, and requires it. It parts
company with a scientific naturalism only in
accepting the authority of instinct or revelation in deciding certain questions of fact,
such as immortality or miracles. It rouses
itself to crush evil, without asking why evil
exists. What could be more intelligible than
that a deity like Jehovah, a giant inhabitant
of the natural world, should be confronted
with rivals, enemies, and rebellious children ?

What could be more intelligible than that
the inertia of matter, or pure chance, or some
contrary purpose, should mar the expression
of any platonic idea exercising its magic
influence over the world ?  For the Greek as
for the Jew the task of morals is the same :
to subdue nature as far as possible to the uses
of the soul, by whatever agencies material or
spiritual may be at hand ; and when a limit
is reached in that direction, to harden and
cauterise the heart in the face of inevitable
evils, opening it wide at the same time to
every sweet influence that may descend to it
from heaven.  Never for a moment was
positive religion entangled in a sophistical
optimism.  Never did it conceive that the
most complete final deliverance and triumph
would *justify* the evils which they abolished.
As William James put it, in his picturesque
manner, if at the last day all creation was
shouting hallelujah and there remained one
cockroach with an unrequited love, *that*
would spoil the universal harmony ; it would
spoil it, he meant, in truth and for the tender
philosopher, but probably not for those
excited saints.  James was thinking chiefly
of the present and future, but the same

scrupulous charity has its application to the past. To remove an evil is not to remove the fact that it has existed. The tears that have been shed were shed in bitterness, even if a remorseful hand afterwards wipes them away. To be patted on the back and given a sugar-plum does not reconcile even a child to a past injustice. And the case is much worse if we are expected to make our heaven out of the foolish and cruel pleasures of contrast, or out of the pathetic offuscation produced by a great relief. Such a heaven would be a lie, like the sardonic heavens of Calvin and Hegel. The existence of any evil anywhere at any time absolutely ruins a total optimism.

Nevertheless philosophers have always had a royal road to complete satisfaction. One of the purest of pleasures, which they cultivate above all others, is the pleasure of understanding. Now, as playwrights and novelists know, the intellect is no less readily or agreeably employed in understanding evil than in understanding good — more so, in fact, if in the intellectual man, besides his intelligence, there is a strain of coarseness, irony, or desire to belittle the good things others possess and he himself has missed. Sometimes the philosopher, even when above all meanness, becomes so devoted a naturalist that he is ashamed to remain a moralist, although this is what he probably was in the beginning; and where all is one vast cataract of events, he feels it would be impertinent of him to divide them censoriously into things that ought to be and things that ought not to be. He may even go one step farther. Awestruck and humbled before the universe, he may insensibly transform his understanding and admiration of it into the assertion that the existence of evil is no evil at all, but that the order of the universe is in every detail necessary and perfect, so that the mere mention of the word evil is blind and blasphemous.

This sentiment, which as much as any other deserves the name of pantheism, is often expressed incoherently and with a false afflatus; but when rationally conceived, as it was by Spinoza, it amounts to this : that good and evil are relations which things bear to the living beings they affect. In itself nothing—much less this whole mixed universe —can be either good or bad ; but the universe

wears the aspect of a good in so far as it
feeds, delights, or otherwise fosters any
creature within it.  If we define the intellect
as the power to see things as they are, it is
clear that in so far as the philosopher is a
pure intellect the universe will be a pure good
to the philosopher; everything in it will
give play to his exclusive passion.  Wisdom
counsels us therefore to become philosophers
and to concentrate our lives as much as
possible in pure intelligence, that we may be
led by it into the ways of peace.  Not that
the universe will be proved thereby to be
intrinsically good (although in the heat of
their intellectual egotism philosophers are
sometimes betrayed into saying so), but that
it will have become in that measure a good
to us, and we shall be better able to live
happily and freely in it.  If intelligibility
appears in things, it does so like beauty or
use, because the mind of man, in so far as it
is adapted to them, finds its just exercise in
their society.

This is an ancient, shrewd, and inex-
pugnable position.  If Royce had been able
to adhere to it consistently, he would have
avoided his gratuitous problem of evil with-

out, I think, doing violence to the sanest element in his natural piety, which was joy in the hard truth, with a touch of humour and scorn in respect to mortal illusions. There was an observant and docile side to him ; and as a child likes to see things work, he liked to see processions of facts marching on ironically, whatever we might say about it.  This was his sense of the power of God. It attached him at first to Spinoza and later to mathematical logic.  No small part of his life-long allegiance to the Absolute responded to this sentiment.

The outlook, however, was complicated and half reversed for him by the transcendental theory of knowledge which he had adopted.  This theory regards all objects, including the universe, as merely terms posited by the will of the thinker, according to a definite grammar of thought native to his mind.  In order that his thoughts may be addressed to any particular object, he must first choose and create it of his own accord ; otherwise his opinions, not being directed upon any object in particular within his ken, cannot be either true or false, whatever picture they may frame.  What any-

thing external may happen to be, when we
do not mean to speak of it, is irrelevant to
our discourse. If, for instance, the real
Royce were not a denizen and product of my
mind — of my deeper self — I could not so
much as have a wrong idea of him. The
need of this initial relevance in our judgements
seems to the transcendentalist to drive all
possible objects into the fold of his secret
thoughts, so that he has two minds, one that
seeks the facts and another that already
possesses or rather constitutes them.

Pantheism, when this new philosophy of
knowledge is adopted, seems at first to lose
its foundations.  There is no longer an
external universe to which to bow ; no little
corner left for us in the infinite where, after
making the great sacrifice, we may build a
safe nest.  The intellect to which we had
proudly reduced ourselves has lost its pre-
eminence ;  it can no longer be called the
faculty of seeing things as they are.  It has
become what psychological critics of intel-
lectualism, such as William James, understand by it : a mass of human propensities
to abstraction, construction, belief, or inference, by which imaginary things and truths

are posited in the service of life. It is therefore on the same plane exactly as passion, music, or æsthetic taste : a mental complication which may be an index to other psychological facts connected with it genetically, but which has no valid intent, no ideal transcendence, no assertive or cognitive function. Intelligence so conceived understands nothing : it is a buzzing labour in the fancy which, by some obscure causation, helps us to live on.

To discredit the intellect, to throw off the incubus of an external reality or truth, was one of the boons which transcendentalism in its beginnings brought to the romantic soul. But although at first the sense of relief (to Fichte, for instance) was most exhilarating, the freedom achieved soon proved illusory : the terrible Absolute had been simply transplanted into the self. You were your own master, and omnipotent ; but you were no less dark, hostile, and inexorable to yourself than the gods of Calvin or of Spinoza had been before. Since every detail of this mock world was your secret work, you were not only wiser but also more criminal than you knew. You were stifled, even more than

formerly, in the arms of nature, in the toils
of your own unaccountable character, which
made your destiny. Royce never recoiled
from paradox or from bitter fact; and he
used to say that a mouse, when tormented
and torn to pieces by a cat, was realising his
own deepest will, since he had sub-consciously
chosen to be a mouse in a world that should
have cats in it. The mouse really, in his
deeper self, wanted to be terrified, clawed,
and devoured. Royce was superficially a
rationalist, with no tenderness for superstition in detail and not much sympathy with
civilised religions; but we see here that in
his heart he was loyal to the aboriginal
principle of all superstition : reverence for
what hurts. He said to himself that
in so far as God was the devil—as daily
experience and Hegelian logic proved was
largely the case—devil-worship was true
religion.

A protest, however, arose in his own mind
against this doctrine. Strong early bonds
attached him to moralism—to the opinion of
the Stoics and of Kant that virtue is the only
good. Yet if virtue were conceived after
their manner, as a heroic and sublimated

attitude of the will, of which the world hardly
afforded any example, how should the whole
whirligig of life be good also ? How should
moralism, that frowns on this wicked world,
be reconciled with pantheism and optimism,
that hug it to their bosom ? By the ingenious if rather melodramatic notion that
we should hug it with a bear's hug, that
virtue consisted (as Royce often put it) in
holding evil by the throat ; so that the world
was good because it was a good world to
strangle, and if we only managed to do so,
the more it deserved strangling the better
world it was. But this Herculean feat must
not be considered as something to accom-
plish once for all ; the labours of Hercules
must be not twelve but infinite, since his
virtue consisted in performing them, and if
he ever rested or was received into Olympus
he would have left virtue—the only good—
behind. The wickedness of the world was
no reason for quitting it ; on the contrary,
it invited us to plunge into all its depths and
live through every phase of it ; virtue was
severe but not squeamish. It lived by endless effort, turbid vitality, and *Sturm und
Drang*. Moralism and an apology for evil

could thus be reconciled and merged in the praises of tragic experience.

This had been the burden of Hegel's philosophy of life, which Royce admired and adopted. Hegel and his followers seem to be fond of imagining that they are moving in a tragedy. But because Aeschylus and Sophocles were great poets, does it follow that life would be cheap if it did not resemble their fables ? The life of tragic heroes is not good ; it is misguided, unnecessary, and absurd. Yet that is what romantic philosophy would condemn us to ; we must all strut and roar. We must lend ourselves to the partisan earnestness of persons and nations calling their rivals villains and themselves heroes; but this earnestness will be of the histrionic German sort, made to order and transferable at short notice from one object to another, since what truly matters is not that we should achieve our ostensible aim (which Hegel contemptuously called ideal) but that we should carry on perpetually, if possible with a *crescendo*, the strenuous experience of living in a gloriously bad world, and always working to reform it, with the comforting speculative assurance that we never can succeed.  We never can succeed, I mean, in rendering reform less necessary or life happier;  but of course in any specific reform we may succeed half the time, thereby sowing the seeds of new and higher evils, to keep the edge of virtue keen.  And in reality we, or the Absolute in us, are succeeding all the time;  the play is always going on, and the play's the thing.

It was inevitable that Royce should have been at home only in this circle of Protestant and German intuitions;  a more refined existence would have seemed to him to elude moral experience.  Although he was born in California he had never got used to the sunshine;  he had never tasted peace. His spirit was that of courage and labour. He was tender in a bashful way, as if in tenderness there was something pathological, as indeed to his sense there was, since he conceived love and loyalty to be divine obsessions refusing to be rationalised;  he saw their essence in the child who clings to an old battered doll rather than accept a new and better one.  Following orthodox tradition in philosophy, he insisted on seeing

reason at the bottom of things as well as
at the top, so that he never could understand either the root or the flower of
anything. He watched the movement of
events as if they were mysterious music,
and instead of their causes and potentialities
he tried to divine their *motif*. On current
affairs his judgements were highly seasoned
and laboriously wise. If anything escaped
him, it was only the simplicity of what is
best. His reward was that he became a
prophet to a whole class of earnest, troubled
people who, having discarded doctrinal religion, wished to think their life worth living
when, to look at what it contained, it might
not have seemed so ; it reassured them to
learn that a strained and joyless existence
was not their unlucky lot, or a consequence
of their solemn folly, but was the necessary
fate of all good men and angels. Royce had
always experienced and seen about him a
groping, burdened, mediocre life ; he had
observed how fortune is continually lying
in ambush for us, in order to bring good
out of evil and evil out of good. In his
age and country all was change, prepara-
tion, hurry, material achievement ; nothing

was an old and sufficient possession; no-
where, or very much in the background, any
leisure, simplicity, security, or harmony.
The whole scene was filled with arts and
virtues which - were merely useful or re-
medial. The most pressing arts, like war
and forced labour, presuppose evil, work immense havoc, and take the place of greater
possible goods. The most indispensable
virtues, like courage and industry, do like-
wise. But these seemed in Royce's world
the only honourable things, and he took
them to be typical of all art and virtue—
a tremendous error. It is very true, however, that in the welter of material existence
no concrete thing can be good or evil in
every respect; and so long as our rough
arts and virtues do more good than harm
we give them honourable names, such as
unselfishness, patriotism, or religion; and
it remains a mark of good breeding among
us to practise them instinctively. But an
absolute love of such forced arts and impure
virtues is itself a vice; it is, as the case
may be, barbarous, vain, or fanatical. It
mistakes something specific—some habit or
emotion which may be or may have been

good in some respect, or under some circumstances the lesser of two evils—for the very
principle of excellence. But good and evil,
like light and shade, are ethereal ; all things,
events, persons, and conventional virtues
are in themselves utterly valueless, save as
an immaterial harmony (of which mind is
an expression) plays about them on occasion,
when their natures meet propitiously, and
bathes them in some tint of happiness or
beauty. This immaterial harmony may be
made more and more perfect ; the difficulties
in the way of perfection, either in man, in
society, or in universal nature, are physical
not logical. Worship of barbarous virtue is
the blackest conservatism ; it shuts the
gate of heaven, and surrenders existence to
perpetual follies and crimes. Moralism itself is a superstition. In its abstract form
it is moral, too moral ; it adores the conventional conscience, or perhaps a morbid
one. In its romantic form, moralism becomes barbarous and actually immoral ; it
obstinately craves action and stress for
their own sake, experience in the gross, and
a good-and-bad way of living.

Royce sometimes conceded that there

might be some pure goods, music, for instance, or mathematics; but the impure
moral goods were better and could not be
spared. Such a concession, however, if it
had been taken to heart, would have ruined
his whole moral philosophy. The romanticist must maintain that *only* what is painful
can be noble and *only* what is lurid bright.
A taste for turbid and contrasted values
would soon seem perverse when once anything perfect had been seen and loved.
Would it not have been better to leave out
the worst of the crimes and plagues that
have heightened the tragic value of the
world? But if so, why stop before we had
deleted them all? We should presently
be horrified at the mere thought of passions
that before had been found necessary by
the barbarous tragedian to keep his audience
awake; and the ear at the same time would
become sensitive to a thousand harmonies
that had been inaudible in the hurly-burly of
romanticism. The romanticist thinks he has
life by virtue of his confusion and torment,
whereas in truth that torment and confusion
are his incipient death, and it is only the
modicum of harmony he has achieved in

his separate faculties that keeps him alive
at all. As Aristotle taught, unmixed harmony would be intensest life. The spheres
might make a sweet and perpetual music,
and a happy God is at least possible.

It was not in this direction, however,
that Royce broke away on occasion from
his Hegelian ethics ; he did so in the direction of ethical dogmatism and downright
sincerity. The deepest thing in him per-
sonally was conscience, firm recognition of
duty, and the democratic and American
spirit of service. He could not adopt a
moral bias histrionically, after the manner
of Hegel or Nietzsche. To those hardened
professionals any rôle was acceptable, the
more commanding the better ; but the
good Royce was like a sensitive amateur,
refusing the rôle of villain, however brilliant
and necessary to the play. In contempt of
his own speculative insight, or in an obedience to it which forgot it for the time being,
he lost himself in his part, and felt that it
was infinitely important to be cast only for
the most virtuous of characters. He retained
inconsistently the Jewish allegiance to a
God essentially the vindicator of only one

of the combatants, not in this world often
the victor ; he could not stomach the providential scoundrels which the bad taste of
Germany, and of Carlyle and Browning,
was wont to glorify. The last notable act
of his life was an illustration of this, when
he uttered a ringing public denunciation of
the sinking of the *Lusitania.* Orthodox
Hegelians might well have urged that here,
if anywhere, was a plain case of the providential function of what, from a finite
merely moral point of view, was an evil in
order to make a higher good possible—the
virtue of German self-assertion and of American self-assertion in antithesis to it, syn-
thesised in the concrete good of war and
victory, or in the perhaps more blessed
good of defeat. What could be more un-
philosophical and *gedankenlos* than the in-
trusion of mere morality into the higher
idea of world-development ? Was not the
Universal Spirit compelled to bifurcate into
just such Germans and just such Americans,
in order to attain self-consciousness by
hating, fighting against, and vanquishing
itself ? Certainly it was American duty
to be angry, as it was German duty to be

ruthless. The Idea liked to see its fighting-
cocks at it in earnest, since that was what
it had bred them for; but both were good
cocks. Villains, as Hegel had observed in
describing Greek tragedy, were not less
self-justified than heroes; they were simply
the heroes of a lower stage of culture.
America and England remained at the stage
of individualism; Germany had advanced
to the higher stage of organisation. Perhaps
this necessary war was destined, through
the apparent defeat of Germany, to bring
England and America up to the German
level. Of course; and yet somehow, on
this occasion, Royce passed over these profound considerations, which life-long habit
must have brought to his lips. A Socratic
demon whispered No, No in his ear; it
would have been better for such things
never to be. The murder of those thousand
passengers was not a providential act, requisite to spread abroad a vitalising war;
it was a crime to execrate altogether. It
would have been better for Hegel, or who-
ever was responsible for it, if a millstone
had been hanged about his neck and he,
and not those little ones, had been drowned

at the bottom of the sea. Of this terrestrial cock-pit Royce was willing to accept the agony, but not the ignominy. The other cock was a wicked bird.

This honest lapse from his logic was habitual with him at the sight of sin, and sin in his eyes was a fearful reality. His conscience spoiled the pantheistic serenity of his system ; and what was worse (for he was perfectly aware of the contradiction) it added a deep, almost remorseful unrest to his hard life. What calm could there be in the double assurance that it was really right that things should be wrong, but that it was really wrong not to strive to right them ? There was no conflict, he once observed, between science and religion, but the real conflict was between religion and morality. There could indeed be no con- flict in his mind between faith and science, because his faith began by accepting all facts and all scientific probabilities in order to face them religiously. But there was an invincible conflict between religion as he conceived it and morality, because morality takes sides and regards one sort of motive and one kind of result as better than another, whereas religion according to him gloried in everything, even in the evil, as fulfilling the will of God. Of course the practice of virtue was not excluded; it was just as needful as evil was in the scheme of the whole; but while the effort of morality was requisite, the judgements of morality were absurd. Now I think we may say that a man who finds himself in such a position has a divided mind, and that while he has wrestled with the deepest questions like a young giant, he has not won the fight. I mean, he has not seen his way to any one of the various possibilities about the nature of things, but has remained entangled, sincerely, nobly, and pathetically, in contrary traditions stronger than himself. In the goodly company of philosophers he is an intrepid martyr.

In metaphysics as in morals Royce perpetually laboured the same points, yet they never became clear; they covered a natural complexity in the facts which his idealism could not disentangle. There was a voluminous confusion in his thought; some clear principles and ultimate possibilities turned up in it, now presenting one face and now

another, like chips carried down a swollen
stream; but the most powerful currents were
·below the surface, and the whole movement
was hard to trace.  He had borrowed from
Hegel a way of conceiving systems of philosophy, and also the elements of his own
thought, which did not tend to clarify them.
He did not think of correcting what incoherence there might remain in any view,
and then holding it in reserve, as one of the
possibilities, until facts should enable us to
decide whether it was true or not.  Instead he clung to the incoherence as if it
had been the heart of the position, in order
to be driven by it to some other position
altogether, so that while every view seemed
to be considered, criticised, and in a measure
retained (since the argument continued on
the same lines, however ill-chosen they might
have been originally), yet justice was never
done to it;  it was never clarified, made
consistent with itself, and then accepted
or rejected in view of the evidence.  Hence
a vicious and perplexing suggestion that
philosophies are bred out of philosophies,
not out of men in the presence of things.
Hence too a sophistical effort to find every-

thing self-contradictory, and in some dis-
quieting way both true and false, as if there
were not an infinite number of perfectly
consistent systems which the world might
have illustrated.

Consider, for instance, his chief and most
puzzling contention, that all minds are parts
of one mind.  It is easy, according to the
meaning we give to the word mind, to render
this assertion clear and true, or clear and
false, or clear and doubtful (because touching unknown facts), or utterly absurd.  It
is obvious that all minds are parts of one
flux or system of experiences, as all bodies
are parts of one system of bodies.  Again,
if mind is identified with its objects, and
people are said to be " of one mind " when
they are thinking of the same thing, it is
certain that many minds are often identical
in part, and they would all be identical with
portions of an omniscient mind that should
perceive all that they severally experienced.
The question becomes doubtful if what we
mean by oneness of mind is unity of type ;
our information or plausible guesses cannot
assure us how many sorts of experience
may exist, or to what extent their develop-

K

ment (when they develop) follows the same lines of evolution. The animals would have to be consulted, and the other planets, and the infinite recesses of time. The strait-jacket which German idealism has provided is certainly far too narrow even for the varieties of human imagination. Finally, the assertion becomes absurd when it is understood to suggest that an actual instance of thinking, in which something, say the existence of America, is absent or denied, can be part of another actual instance of thinking in which it is present and asserted. But this whole method of treating the matter—and we might add anything that observation might warrant us in adding about multiple personalities—would leave out the problem that agitated Royce and that bewildered his readers. He wanted all minds to be one in some way which should be logically and morally necessary, and which yet, as he could not help feeling, was morally and logically impossible.

For pure transcendentalism, which was Royce's technical method, the question does not arise at all. Transcendentalism is an attitude or a point of view rather than a system. Its Absolute is thinking " as such," wherever thought may exert itself. The notion that there are separate instances of thought is excluded, because space, time, and number belong to the visionary world posited by thought, not to the function of thinking; individuals are figments of con- structive fancy, as are material objects. The stress of moral being is the same wher- ever it may fall, and there are no finite selves, or relations between thinkers; also no infinite self, because on this principle the Absolute is not an existent being, a psychological monster, but a station or office; its essence is a task. Actual think- ing is therefore never a part of the Absolute, but always the Absolute itself. Thinkers, finite or infinite, would be existing persons or masses of feelings; such things are dreamt of only. *Any* system of existences, *any* truth or matter of fact waiting to be recognised, contradicts the transcendental insight and stultifies it. The all-inclusive mind is my mind as I think, mind in its living function, and beyond that philosophy cannot go.

Royce, however, while often reasoning on this principle, was incapable of not going beyond it, or of always remembering it.  He could not help believing that constructive fancy not only feigns individuals and instances of thought, but is actually seated in them.  The Absolute, for instance, must be not merely the abstract subject or transcendental self in all of us (although it was that too), but an actual synthetic universal mind, the God of Aristotle and of Christian theology.  Nor was it easy for Royce, a sincere soul and a friend of William James, not to be a social realist; I mean, not to admit that there are many collateral human minds, in temporal existential relations to one another, any of which may influence another, but never supplant it nor materially include it.  Finite experience was not a mere element in infinite experience; it was a tragic totality in itself.  I was not God looking at myself, I was myself looking for God.  Yet this strain was utterly incompatible with the principles of transcendentalism; it turned philosophy into a simple anticipation of science, if not into an indulgence in literary psychology.  Knowledge would then have been only faith leaping across the chasm of coexistence and guessing

the presence and nature of what surrounds
us by some hint of material influence or
brotherly affinity.  Both the credulity and
the finality which such naturalism implies
were offensive to Royce, and contrary to his
sceptical and mystical instincts.  Was there
some middle course ?

The audience in a theatre stand in a
transcendental relation to the persons and
events in the play.  The performance may
take place to-day and last one hour, while
the fable transports us to some heroic epoch
or to an age that never existed, and stretches
through days and perhaps years of fancied
time.  Just so transcendental thinking,
while actually timeless and not distributed
among persons, might survey infinite time
and rehearse the passions and thoughts of
a thousand characters.  Thought, after all,
needs objects, however fictitious and ideal
they may be ; it could not think if it thought
nothing.  This indispensable world of appearance is far more interesting than the
reality that evokes it ; the qualities and
divisions found in the appearance diversify
the monotonous function of pure thinking
and render it concrete.  Instances of thought

and particular minds may thus be introduced consistently into a transcendental system, provided they are distinguished not by their own times and places, but only by their themes. The transcendental mind would be a pure poet, with no earthly life, but living only in his works, and in the times and persons of his fable. This view, firmly and consistently held, would deserve the name of absolute idealism, which Royce liked to give to his own system. But he struggled to fuse it with social realism, with which it is radically incompatible. Particular minds and the whole process of time, for absolute idealism, are *ideas* only ; they are thought of and surveyed, they never think or lapse actually. For this reason genuine idealists can speak so glibly of the mind of a nation or an age. It is just as real and unreal to them as the mind of an individual ; for within the human individual they can trace unities that run through and beyond him, so that parts of him, identical with parts of other people, form units as living as himself ; for it is all a web of themes, not a concourse of existences. This is the very essence and pride of idealism,

that knowledge is not knowledge of the
world but is the world itself, and that the
units of discourse, which are interwoven and
crossed units, are the only individuals in
being. You may call them persons, because
" person " means a mask ; but you cannot
call them souls. They are knots in the web
of history. They are words in their con-
text, and the only spirit in them is the sense
they have for me.

Royce, however, in saying all this, also
wished not to say it, and his two thick volumes
on *The World and the Individual* leave their
subject wrapped in utter obscurity. Perceiv-
ing the fact when he had finished, he very
characteristically added a " Supplementary
Essay " of a hundred more pages, in finer
print, in which to come to the point.
Imagine, he said, an absolutely exhaustive
map of England spread out upon English
soil. The map would be a part of England,
yet would reproduce every feature of England, including itself ; so that the map
would reappear on a smaller scale within
itself an infinite number of times, like a
mirror reflected in a mirror. In this way
we might be individuals within a larger

individual, and no less actual and complete
than he. Does this solve the problem ? If
we take the illustration as it stands, there is
still only one individual in existence, the
material England, all the maps being parts
of its single surface ; nor will it at all resemble the maps, since it will be washed by
the sea and surrounded by foreign nations,
and not, like the maps, by other Englands
enveloping it. If, on the contrary, we equalise
the status of all the members of the series,
by making it infinite in both directions, then
there would be no England at all, but only
map within map of England. There would
be no absolute mind inclusive but not
included, and the Absolute would be the
series as a whole, utterly different from
any of its members. It would be a series
while they were maps, a truth while they
were minds ; and if the Absolute from the
beginning had been regarded as a truth
only, there never would have been any
difficulty in the existence of individuals
under it. Moreover, if the individuals are
all exactly alike, does not their exact similarity defeat the whole purpose of the
speculation, which was to vindicate the equal

reality of the whole and of its *limited* parts ?
And if each of us, living through infinite time,
goes through precisely the same experiences
as every one else, why this vain repetition ?
Is it not enough for this insatiable world to
live its life once ?   Why not admit solipsism
and be true to the transcendental method ?
Because of conscience and good sense ?   But
then the infinite series of maps is useless,
England is herself again, and the prospect
opens before us of an infinite number of
supplementary essays.

Royce sometimes felt that he might have
turned his hand to other things than philosophy.   He once wrote a novel, and its
want of success was a silent disappointment
to him.  Perhaps he might have been a
great musician.  Complexity, repetitions,
vagueness, endlessness are hardly virtues
in writing or thinking, but in music they
might have swelled and swelled into a real
sublimity, all the more that he was patient,
had a voluminous meandering memory, and
loved technical devices.  But rather than
a musician—for he was no artist—he resembled some great-hearted mediæval
peasant visited by mystical promptings,

whom the monks should have adopted and allowed to browse among their theological folios ; a Duns Scotus earnest and studious to a fault, not having the lightness of soul to despise those elaborate sophistries, yet minded to ferret out their secret for himself and walk by his inward light. His was a gothic and scholastic spirit, intent on devising and solving puzzles, and honouring God in systematic works, like the coral insect or the spider ; eventually creating a fabric that in its homely intricacy and fulness arrested and moved the heart, the web of it was so vast, and so full of mystery and yearning.

# CHAPTER V

A QUESTION which is curious in itself and may become important in the future is this : How has migration to the new world affected philosophical ideas ? At first sight we might be tempted, perhaps, to dismiss this question altogether, on the ground that no such effect is discernible. For what do we find in America in the guise of philosophy ? In the background, the same Protestant theology as in Europe and the same Catholic theology ; on the surface, the same adoption of German idealism, the same vogue of evolution, the same psychology becoming metaphysics, and lately the same revival of a mathematical or logical realism. In no case has the first expression of these various tendencies appeared in America, and no original system that I know of has arisen there. It would

seem, then, that in philosophy, as in letters
generally, polite America has continued the
common tradition of Christendom, in paths
closely parallel to those followed in England ;
and that modern speculation, which is so very
sensitive to changed times, is quite indifferent
to distinctions of place.

Perhaps ; but I say advisedly *polite*
America, for without this qualification what
I have been suggesting would hardly be true.
Polite America carried over its household
gods from puritan England in a spirit of con-
secration, and it has always wished to remain
in communion with whatever its conscience
might value in the rest of the world.   Yet
it has been cut off by distance and by revolutionary prejudice against things ancient or
foreign ;  and it has been disconcerted at the
same time by the insensible shifting of the
ground under its feet :  it has suffered from
in-breeding and anæmia.   On the other hand,
a crude but vital America has sprung up
from the soil, undermining, feeding, and
transforming the America of tradition.

This young America was originally composed of all the prodigals, truants, and adventurous spirits that the colonial families

produced : it was fed continually by the younger generation, born in a spacious, half-empty world, tending to forget the old straitened morality and to replace it by another, quite jovially human. This truly native America was reinforced by the miscellany of Europe arriving later, not in the hope of founding a godly commonwealth, but only of prospering in an untrammelled one. The horde of immigrants eagerly accepts the external arrangements and social spirit of American life, but never hears of its original austere principles, or relegates them to the same willing oblivion as it does the constraints which it has just escaped—Jewish, Irish, German, Italian, or whatever they may be. We should be seriously deceived if we overlooked for a moment the curious and complex relation between these two Americas.

Let me give one illustration. Professor Norton, the friend of Carlyle, of Burne-Jones, and of Matthew Arnold, and, for the matter of that, the friend of everybody, a most urbane, learned, and exquisite spirit, was descended from a long line of typical New England divines : yet he was loudly accused, in public and in private, of being un-American.

On the other hand, a Frenchman of ripe judgement, who knew him perfectly, once said to me : " Norton wouldn't like to hear it, but he is a terrible Yankee." Both judgements were well grounded. Professor Norton's mind was deeply moralised, discriminating, and sad ; and these qualities rightly seemed American to the French observer of New England, but they rightly seemed un-American to the politician from Washington.

Philosophical opinion in America is of course rooted in the genteel tradition. It is either inspired by religious faith, and designed to defend it, or else it is created somewhat artificially in the larger universities, by deliberately proposing problems which, without being very pressing to most Americans, are supposed to be necessary problems of thought. Yet if you expected academic philosophers in America, because the background of their minds seems perfunctory, to resemble academic philosophers elsewhere, you would be often mistaken. There is no prig's paradise in those regions. Many of the younger professors of philosophy are no longer the sort of persons that might as well have been clergymen or schoolmasters : they

have rather the type of mind of a doctor, an
engineer, or a social reformer; the wide-
awake young man who can do most things
better than old people, and who knows it.
He is less eloquent and apostolic than the
older generation of philosophers, very professional in tone and conscious of his *Fach*;
not that he would deny for a moment the
many-sided ignorance to which nowadays we
are all reduced, but that he thinks he can get
on very well without the things he ignores.
His education has been more pretentious
than thorough; his style is deplorable;
social pressure and his own great eagerness
have condemned him to over-work, committee
meetings, early marriage, premature author-
ship, and lecturing two or three times a day
under forced draught. He has no peace in
himself, no window open to a calm horizon,
and in his heart perhaps little taste for mere
scholarship or pure speculation. Yet, like
the plain soldier staggering under his clumsy
equipment, he is cheerful; he keeps his faith
in himself and in his allotted work, puts up
with being toasted only on one side, remains
open - minded, whole - hearted, appreciative,
helpful, confident of the future of goodness

and of science. In a word, he is a cell in that
teeming democratic body; he draws from
its warm, contagious activities the sanctions
of his own life and, less consciously, the spirit
of his philosophy.

It is evident that such minds will have
but a loose hold on tradition, even on the
genteel tradition in American philosophy.
Not that in general they oppose or dislike it;
their alienation from it is more radical; they
forget it. Religion was the backbone of that
tradition, and towards religion, in so far as
it is a private sentiment or presumption,
they feel a tender respect; but in so far as
religion is a political institution, seeking to
coerce the mind and the conscience, one
would think they had never heard of it.
They feel it is as much every one's right to
choose and cherish a religion as to choose and
cherish a wife, without having his choice
rudely commented upon in public. Hitherto
America has been the land of universal good-
will, confidence in life, inexperience of poisons.
Until yesterday it believed itself immune
from the hereditary plagues of mankind. It
could not credit the danger of being suffocated
or infected by any sinister principle. The

more errors and passions were thrown into
the melting-pot, the more certainly would
they neutralise one another and would truth
come to the top.  Every system was met
with a frank gaze.  " Come on," people
seemed to say to it, " show us what you are
good for.  We accept no claims ; we ask for
no credentials ; we just give you a chance.
Plato, the Pope, and Mrs. Eddy shall have
one vote each."  After all, I am not sure
that this toleration without deference is not
a cruel test for systematic delusions : it lets
the daylight into the stage.

Philosophic tradition in America has
merged almost completely in German idealism.  In a certain sense this system did not
need to be adopted : something very like
it had grown up spontaneously in New
England in the form of transcendentalism
and unitarian theology.  Even the most
emancipated and positivistic of the latest
thinkers—pragmatists, new realists, pure empiricists—have been bred in the atmosphere
of German idealism ; and this fact should
not be forgotten in approaching their views.
The element of this philosophy which has
sunk deepest, and which is reinforced by the

L

influence of psychology, is the critical attitude
towards knowledge, subjectivism, withdrawal
into experience, on the assumption that
experience is something substantial. Experience was regarded by earlier empiricists
as a method for making real discoveries, a
safer witness than reasoning to what might
exist in nature ; but now experience is taken
to be in itself the only real existence, the
ultimate object that all thought and theory
must regard. This empiricism does not look
to the building up of science, but rather to a
more thorough criticism and disintegration
of conventional beliefs, those of empirical
science included. It is in the intrepid prose-
cution of this criticism and disintegration
that American philosophy has won its wings.

It may seem a strange Nemesis that a
critical philosophy, which on principle reduces
everything to the consciousness of it, should
end by reducing consciousness itself to other
things ; yet the path of this boomerang is
not hard to trace. The word consciousness
originally meant what Descartes called
thought or cogitation—the faculty which
attention has of viewing together objects
which may belong together neither in their

logical essence nor in their natural existence.
It colours events with memories and facts
with emotions, and adds images to words.
This synthetic and transitive function of
consciousness is a positive fact about it, to
be discovered by study, like any other somewhat recondite fact.  You will discover it if
you institute a careful comparison and contrast between the way things hang together
in thought and the way they hang together
in nature.  To have discerned the wonderful
perspectives both of imagination and of will
seems to me the chief service done to philosophy by Kant and his followers.  It is the
positive, the non-malicious element in their
speculation ;  and in the midst of their
psychologism in logic and their egotism about
nature and history, consciousness seems to
be the one province of being which they have
thrown true light upon.  But just because
this is a positive province of being, an actual
existence to be discovered and dogmatically
believed in, it is not what a malicious criticism
of knowledge can end with.  Not the nature
of consciousness, but the data of consciousness, are what the critic must fall back upon
in the last resort ;  and Hume had been in

this respect a more penetrating critic than
Kant.   One cannot, by inspecting consciousness, find consciousness itself as a passive
datum, because consciousness is cogitation ;
one can only take note of the immediate
objects of consciousness, in such private
perspective as sense or imagination may
present.

Philosophy seems to be richer in theories
than in words to express them in ; and much
confusion results from the necessity of using
old terms in new meanings.   In this way,
when consciousness is disregarded, in the
proper sense of cogitation, the name of consciousness can be transferred to the stream
of objects immediately present to consciousness ; so that consciousness comes to signify
the evolving field of appearances unrolled
before any person.

This equivocation is favoured by the allied
ambiguity of an even commoner term, idea.
It is plausible to say that consciousness is a
stream of ideas, because an idea may mean
an opinion, a cogitation, a view taken of
some object.   And it is also plausible to say
that ideas are objects of consciousness, because
an idea may mean an image, a passive datum.

Passive data may be of any sort you like—
things, qualities, relations, propositions—but
they are never cogitations ; and to call *them*
consciousness or components of consciousness
is false and inexcusable.  The ideas that may
be so called are not these passive objects, but
active thoughts.  Indeed, when the psychological critic has made this false step, he
is not able to halt :  his method will carry
him presently from this position to one even
more paradoxical.

Is memory knowledge of a past that is
itself absent and dead, or is it a present
experience ?  A complete philosophy would
doubtless reply that it is both ;  but psychological criticism can take cognisance of
memory only as a mass of present images and
presumptions.  The experience remembered
may indeed be exactly recovered and be
present again ;  but the fact that it was
present before cannot possibly be given now ;
it can only be suggested and believed.

It is evident, therefore, that the historical
order in which data flow is not contained
bodily in any one of them.  This order is
conceived ;  the hypothesis is framed instinctively and instinctively credited, but it is

only an hypothesis.  And it is often wrong, as is proved by all the constitutional errors of memory and legend.  Belief in the order of our personal experiences is accordingly just as dogmatic, daring, and realistic as the parallel belief in a material world. The psychological critic must attribute both beliefs to a mere tendency to feign ; and if he is true to his method he must discard the notion that the objects of consciousness are arranged in psychological sequences, making up separate minds.  In other words, he must discard the notion of consciousness, not only in the sense of thought or cogitation, but in the sense he himself had given it of a stream of ideas.  Actual objects, he will now admit, not without a certain surprise, are not ideas at all : they do not lie in the mind (for there is no mind to be found) but in the medium that observably surrounds them.  Things are just what they seem to be, and to say they are consciousness or compose a consciousness is absurd.  The so-called appearances, according to a perfected criticism of knowledge, are nothing private or internal ; they are merely those portions of external objects which from time to time impress themselves on somebody's organs of ·sense and are responded to by his nervous system.

Such is the doctrine of the new American realists, in whose devoted persons the logic of idealism has worked itself out and appropriately turned idealism itself into its opposite. Consciousness, they began by saying, is merely a stream of ideas ; but then ideas are merely the parts of objects which happen to appear to a given person ; but again, a person (for all you or he can discover) is nothing but his body and those parts of other objects which appear to him ; and, finally, to appear, in any discoverable sense, cannot be to have a ghostly sort of mental existence, but merely to be reacted upon by an animal body. Thus we come to the conclusion that objects alone exist, and that consciousness is a name for certain segments or groups of these objects.

I think we may conjecture why this startling conclusion, that consciousness does not exist, a conclusion suggested somewhat hurriedly by William James, has found a considerable echo in America, and why the system of Avenarius, which makes in the same direction, has been studied there sympathetically. To deny consciousness is to deny a pre-requisite to the obvious, and to leave the obvious standing alone. That is a relief to an overtaxed and self-impeded generation ; it seems a blessed simplification. It gets rid of the undemocratic notion that by being very reflective, circumspect, and subtle you might discover something that most people do not see. They can go on more merrily with their work if they believe that by being so subtle, circumspect, and reflective you would only discover a mare's nest. The elimination of consciousness not only restores the obvious, but proves all parts of the obvious to be equally real. Not only colours, beauties, and passions, but all things formerly suspected of being creatures of thought, such as laws, relations, and abstract qualities, now become components of the existing object, since there is no longer any mental vehicle by which they might have been created and interposed. The young American is thus reassured : his joy in living and learning is no longer chilled by the contempt which idealism used to cast on nature for being imaginary and on science for being intellectual. All fictions and all abstractions are now declared to be parcels of the objective world ; it will suffice to live on, to live forward, in order to see everything as it really is.

If we look now at these matters from a slightly different angle, we shall find psychological criticism transforming the notion of truth much as it has transformed the notion of consciousness. In the first place, there is a similar ambiguity in the term. The truth properly means the sum of all true propositions, what omniscience would assert, the whole ideal system of qualities and relations which the world has exemplified or will exemplify. The truth is all things seen under the form of eternity. In this sense, a psychological criticism cannot be pertinent to the truth at all, the truth not being anything psychological or human. It is an ideal realm of being properly enough not discussed by psychologists ; yet so far as I know it is denied by nobody, not even by Protagoras or the pragmatists. If Protagoras said that whatever appears to any man at any moment is true, he doubtless meant true on that subject, true of that appearance : because for a sensualist objects do not extend beyond what he sees of them, so that each of his

perceptions defines its whole object and is
infallible.  But in that case the truth about
the universe is evidently that it is composed
of these various sensations, each carrying an
opinion impossible for it to abandon or to,
revise, since to revise the opinion would
simply be to bring a fresh object into view.
The truth would further be that these sensations and opinions stand to one another in
certain definite relations of diversity, succession, duration, *et cætera*, whether any of
them happens to assert these relations or
not.  In the same way, I cannot find that
our contemporary pragmatists, in giving
their account of what truth is (in a different
and quite abstract sense of the word truth),
have ever doubted, or so much as noticed,
what in all their thinking they evidently
assume to be the actual and concrete truth :
namely, that there are many states of mind,
many labouring opinions more or less useful
and good, which actually lead to others, more
or less expected and satisfactory.  Surely
every pragmatist, like every thinking man,
always assumes the reality of an actual truth,
comprehensive and largely undiscovered, of
which he claims to be reporting a portion.

What he rather confusingly calls truth, and wishes to reduce to a pragmatic function, is not this underlying truth, the sum of all true propositions, but merely the abstract quality which all true propositions must have in common, to be called true. By truth he means only correctness. The possibility of correctness in an idea is a great puzzle to him, on account of his idealism, which identifies ideas with their objects ; and he asks himself how an idea can ever come to be correct or incorrect, as if it referred to something beyond itself.

The fact is, of course, that an idea can be correct or incorrect only if by the word idea we mean not a datum but an opinion ; and the abstract relation of correctness, by virtue of which any opinion is true, is easily stated. An opinion is true if what it is talking about is constituted as the opinion asserts it to be constituted. To test this correctness may be difficult or even impossible in particular cases ; in the end we may be reduced to believing on instinct that our fundamental opinions are true ; for instance, that we are living through time, and that · the past and future are not, as a consistent

idealism would assert, mere notions in the
present. But what renders such instinctive
opinions true, if they are true, is the fact
affirmed being as it is affirmed to be. It is
not a question of similarity or derivation
between a passive datum and a hidden
object; it is a question of identity between
the fact asserted and the fact existing. If
an opinion could not freely leap to its object,
no matter how distant or hypothetical, and
assert something of that chosen object, an
opinion could not be so much as wrong;
for it would not be an opinion about
anything.

Psychologists, however, are not concerned
with what an opinion asserts logically, but
only with what it is existentially; they are
asking what existential relations surround
an idea when it is called true which are absent
when it is called false. Their problem is
frankly insoluble; for it requires us to discover what makes up the indicative force
of an idea which by hypothesis is a passive
datum; as if a grammarian should inquire
how a noun in the accusative case could be
a verb in the indicative mood.

It was not idly that William James

dedicated his book on Pragmatism to the memory of John Stuart Mill. The principle of psychological empiricism is to look for the elements employed in thinking, and to conclude that thought is nothing but those elements arranged in a certain order. It is true .that since the days of Mill analysis has somewhat extended the inventory of these elements, so as to include among simples, besides the data of the five senses, such things as feelings of relation, sensations of movement, vague ill-focused images, and perhaps even telepathic and instinctive intuitions. But some series or group of these immediate data, kept in their crude immediacy, must according to this method furnish the whole answer to our question : the supposed power of an idea to have an object beyond itself, or to be true of any other fact, must be merely a name for a certain position which the given element occupies in relation to other elements in the routine of experience. Knowledge and truth must be forms of contiguity and succession.'

We must not be surprised, under these circumstances, if the problem is shifted, and another somewhat akin to it takes its place,

with which the chosen method can really
cope.  This subterfuge is not voluntary ;  it
is an instinctive effect of fidelity to a point
of view which has its special validity, though
naturally not applicable in every sphere.  We
do not observe that politicians abandon
their party when it happens to have brought
trouble upon the country ;  their destiny as
politicians is precisely to make effective all
the consequences, good or evil, which their
party policy may involve.  So it would be
too much to expect a school of philosophers
to abandon their method because there are
problems it cannot solve ;  their business is
rather to apply their method to everything
to which it can possibly be applied ;  and
when they have reached that limit, the very
most we can ask, if they are superhumanly
modest and wise, is that they should
make way gracefully for another school of
philosophers.

Now there is a problem, not impossible
to confuse with the problem of correctness
in ideas, with which psychological criticism
can really deal ;  it is the question of the
relation between a sign and the thing signified.
Of this relation a genuinely empirical account

can be given; both terms are objects of
experience, present or eventual, and the
passage between them is made in time by an
experienced transition. Nor need the signs
which lead to a particular object be always
the same, or of one sort; an object may
be designated and announced unequivocally
by a verbal description, without any direct
image, or by images now of one sense and
now of another, or by some external relation,
such as its place, or by its proper name, if
it possesses one; and these designations all
convey knowledge of it and may be true
signs, if in yielding to their suggestion we
are brought eventually to the object meant.

Here, if I am not mistaken, is the genuine
application of what the pragmatists call their
theory of truth. It concerns merely what
links a sign to the thing signified, and renders
it a practical substitute for the same. But
this empirical analysis of signification has
been entangled with more or less hazardous
views about truth, such as that an idea is
true so long as it is believed to be true, or
that it is true if it is good and useful, or that
it is not true until it is verified. This last
suggestion shows what strange reversals a

wayward personal philosophy may be subject to. Empiricism used to mean reliance on the past; now apparently all empirical truth regards only the future, since truth is said to arise by the verification of some presumption. Presumptions about the past can evidently never be verified; at best they may be corroborated by fresh presumptions about the past, equally dependent for their truth on a verification which in the nature of the case is impossible. At this point the truly courageous empiricist will perhaps say that the real past only means the ideas of the past which we shall form in the future. Consistency is a jewel; and, as in the case of other jewels, we may marvel at the price that some people will pay for it. In any case, we are led to this curious result : that radical empiricism ought to deny that any idea of the past can be true at all.

Such dissolving views, really somewhat like those attributed to Protagoras, do not rest on sober psychological analysis : they express rather a certain impatience and a certain despairing democracy in the field of opinion. Great are the joys of haste and of radicalism, and young philosophers must not be deprived of them. We maỳ the more justly pass over these small scandals of pragmatism in that William James aǹd his American disciples have hardly cared to defend them, but have turned decidedly in the direction of a universal objectivism.

The spirit of these radical views is not at all negative : it is hopeful, revolutionary, inspired entirely by love of certitude and clearness. It is very sympathetic to science, in so far as science is a personal pursuit and a personal experience, rather than a body of doctrine with moral implications. It is very close to nature, as the lover of nature understands the word. If it denies the existence of the cognitive energy and the colouring medium of mind, it does so only in a formal sense ; all the colours with which that medium endows the world remain painted upon it ; and all the perspectives and ideal objects of thought are woven into the texture of things. Not, I think, intelligibly or in a coherent fashion ; for this new realism is still immature, and if it is ever rendered adequate it will doubtless seem much less original. My point is that in its denial of mind it has no bias against things

M

intellectual, and if it refuses to admit ideas or even sensations, it does not blink the sensible or ideal objects which ideas and sensations reveal, but rather tries to find a new and (as it perhaps thinks) a more honourable place for them; they are not regarded as spiritual radiations from the natural world, but as parts of its substance.

This may have the ring of materialism; but the temper and faith of these schools are not materialistic. Systematic materialism is one of the philosophies of old age. It is a conviction that may overtake a few shrewd and speculative cynics, who have long observed their own irrationality and that of the world, and have divined its cause; by such men materialism may be embraced without reserve, in all its rigour and pungency. But the materialism of youth is part of a simple faith in sense and in science; it is not exclusive; it admits the co-operation of any other forces—divine, magical, formal, or vital—if appearances anywhere seem to manifest them. The more we interpret the ambiguities or crudities of American writers in this sense, the less we shall misunderstand them.

It seems, then, that the atmosphere of the
new world has already affected philosophy
in two ways. In the first place, it has accél-
erated and rendered fearless the disintegration
of conventional categories ; a disintegration
on which modern philosophy has always
been at work, and which has precipitated its
successive phases. In the second place, the
younger cosmopolitan America has favoured
the impartial assemblage and mutual con-
frontation of all sorts of ideas. It has produced, in intellectual matters, a sort of
happy watchfulness and insecurity. Never
was the human mind master of so many facts
and sure of so few principles. Will this
suspense and fluidity of thought crystallise
into some great new system ? Positive gifts
of imagination and moral heroism are requisite to make a great philosopher, gifts
which must come from the gods and not
from circumstances. But if the genius should
arise, this vast collection of suggestions and
this radical analysis of presumptions which
he will find in America may keep him from
going astray. Nietzsche said that the earth
has been a mad-house long enough. Without
contradicting him we might perhaps soften

the expression, and say that philosophy has been long enough an asylum for enthusiasts. It is time for it to become less solemn and more serious. We may be frightened at first to learn on what thin ice we have been skating, in speculation as in government; but we shall not be in a worse plight for knowing it, only wiser to-day and perhaps safer to-morrow.

# CHAPTER VI

THE language and traditions common to
England and America are like other family
bonds : they draw kindred together at the
greater crises in life, but they also occasion
at times a little friction and fault-finding.
The groundwork of the two societies is so
similar, that each nation, feeling almost at
home with the other, and almost able to
understand its speech, may instinctively
resent what hinders it from feeling at home
altogether. Differences will tend to seem
anomalies that have slipped in by mistake
and through somebody's fault. Each will
judge the other by his own standards, not
feeling, as in the presence of complete
foreigners, that he must make an effort of
imagination and put himself in another
man's shoes.

In matters of morals, manners, and art,
the danger of comparisons is not merely
that they may prove invidious, by ranging
qualities in an order of merit which might
wound somebody's vanity; the danger is
rather that comparisons may distort com-
prehension, because in truth good qualities
are all different in kind, and free lives are
different in spirit. Comparison is the expedient of those who cannot reach the heart
of the things compared; and no philosophy
is more external and egotistical than that
which places the essence of a thing in its
relation to something else. In reality, at
the centre of every natural being there is
something individual and incommensurable,
a seed with its native impulses and aspirations, shaping themselves as best they can
in their given environment. Variation is
a consequence of freedom, and the slight
but radical diversity of souls in turn makes
freedom requisite. Instead of instituting in
his mind any comparisons between the
United States and other nations, I would
accordingly urge the reader to forget himself
and, in so far as such a thing may be possible
for him or for me, to transport himself ideally

with me into the outer circumstances of American life, the better to feel its inner temper, and to see how inevitably the American shapes his feelings and judgements, honestly reporting all things as they appear from his new and unobstructed station.

I speak of the American in the singular, as if there were not millions of them, north and south, east and west, of both sexes, of all ages, and of various races, professions, and religions. Of course the one American I speak of is mythical ; but to speak in parables is inevitable in such a subject, and it is perhaps as well to do so frankly. There is a sort of poetic ineptitude in all human discourse when it tries to deal with natural and existing things. Practical men may not notice it, but in fact human discourse is intrinsically addressed not to natural existing things but to ideal essences, poetic or logical terms which thought may define and play with. When fortune or necessity diverts our attention from this congenial ideal sport to crude facts and pressing issues, we turn our frail poetic ideas into symbols for those terrible irruptive things. In that paper money of our own stamping, the legal tender

of the mind, we are obliged to reckon all the
movements and values of the world.  The
universal American I speak of is one of these
symbols ;  and I should be still speaking in
symbols and creating moral units and a false
simplicity, if I spoke of classes pedantically
subdivided, or individuals ideally integrated
and defined.  As it happens, the symbolic
American can be made largely adequate to
the facts ;  because, if there are immense
differences between individual Americans—
for some Americans are black—yet there is
a great uniformity in their environment,
customs, temper, and thoughts.  They have
all been uprooted from their several soils and
ancestries and plunged together into one
vortex, whirling irresistibly in a space otherwise quite empty.  To be an American is of
itself almost a moral condition, an education,
and a career.  Hence a single ideal figment
can cover a large part of what each American
is in his character, and almost the whole of
what most Americans are in their social
outlook and political judgements.

The discovery of the new world exercised
a sort of selection among the inhabitants of
Europe.  All the colonists, except the negroes,

were voluntary exiles. The fortunate, the deeply rooted, and the lazy remained at home; the wilder instincts or dissatisfaction of others tempted them beyond the horizon. The American is accordingly the most adventurous, or the descendant of the most adventurous, of Europeans. It is in his blood to be socially a radical, though perhaps not intellectually. What has existed in the past, especially in the remote past, seems to him not only not authoritative, but irrelevant, inferior, and outworn. He finds it rather a sorry waste of time to think about the past at all. But his enthusiasm for the future is profound; he can conceive of no more decisive way of recommending an opinion or a practice than to say that it is what everybody is coming to adopt. This expectation of what he approves, or approval of what he expects, makes up his optimism. It is the necessary faith of the pioneer.

Such a temperament is, of course, not maintained in the nation merely by inheritance. Inheritance notoriously tends to restore the average of a race, and plays incidentally many a trick of atavism. What maintains this temperament and makes it

children are sacred, business is sacred,
America is sacred, Masonic lodges and college
clubs are sacred.  This feeling grows out of
the good opinion he wishes to have of these
things, and serves to maintain it.  If he did
not regard all these things as sacred he might
come to doubt sometimes if they were wholly
good.  Of this kind, too, is the idealism of
single ladies in reduced circumstances who
can see the soul of beauty in ugly things, and
are perfectly happy because their old dog has
such pathetic eyes, their minister is so
eloquent, their garden with its three sun-
flowers is so pleasant, their dead friends were
so devoted, and their distant relations are
so rich.

Consider now the great emptiness of
America: not merely the primitive physical
emptiness, surviving in some regions, and
the continental spacing of the chief natural
features, but also the moral emptiness of a
settlement where men and even houses are
easily moved about, and no one, almost, lives
where he was born or believes what he has
been taught.  Not that the American has
jettisoned these impedimenta in anger; they
have simply slipped from him as he moves.

Great empty spaces bring a sort of freedom
to both soul and body. You may pitch
your tent where you will; or if ever you
decide to build anything, it can be in a style
of your own devising. You have room,
fresh materials, few models, and no critics.
You trust your own experience, not only
because you must, but because you find you
may do so safely and prosperously; the
forces that determine fortune are not yet
too complicated for one man to explore.
Your detachable condition makes you lavish
with money and cheerfully experimental;
you lose little if you lose all, since you remain
completely yourself. At the same time your
absolute initiative gives you practice in
coping with novel situations, and in being
original; it teaches you shrewd management.
Your life and mind will become dry and
direct, with few decorative flourishes. In
your works everything will be stark and
pragmatic; you will not understand why
anybody should make those little sacrifices
to instinct or custom which we call grace.
The fine arts will seem to you academic
luxuries, fit to amuse the ladies, like Greek
and Sanskrit; for while you will perfectly

appreciate generosity in men's purposes, you
will not admit that the execution of these
purposes can be anything but business. Unfortunately the essence of the fine arts is that
the execution should be generous too, and
delightful in itself; therefore the fine arts
will suffer, not so much in their express professional pursuit—for then they become
practical tasks and a kind of business—as in
that diffused charm which qualifies all human
action when men are artists by nature.
Elaboration, which is something to accom-
plish, will be preferred to simplicity, which
is something to rest in ; manners will suffer
somewhat ; speech will suffer horribly. For
the American the urgency of his novel attack
upon matter, his zeal in gathering its fruits,
precludes meanderings in primrose paths ;
devices must be short cuts, and symbols
must be mere symbols. If his wife wants
luxuries, of course she may have them ; and
if he has vices, that can be provided for too ;
but they must all be set down under those
headings in his ledgers.

At the same time, the American is
imaginative ; for where life is intense,
imagination is intense also. Were he not

imaginative he would not live so much in
the future. But his imagination is practical,
and the future it forecasts is immediate ; it
works with the clearest and least ambiguous
terms known to his experience, in terms of
number, measure, contrivance, economy, and
speed. He is an idealist working on matter.
Understanding as he does the material potentialities of things, he is successful in invention,
conservative in reform, and quick in emergen-
cies. All his life he jumps into the train
after it has started and jumps out before it
has stopped ; and he never once gets left
behind, or breaks a leg. There is an enthusiasm in his sympathetic handling of material
forces which goes far to cancel the illiberal
character which it might otherwise assume.
The good workman hardly distinguishes his
artistic intention from the potency in himself
and in things which is about to realise that
intention. Accordingly his ideals fall into
the form of premonitions and prophecies ;
and his studious prophecies often come true.
So do the happy workmanlike ideals of the
American. When a poor boy, perhaps, he
dreams of an education, and presently he
gets an education, or at least a degree ; he

dreams of growing rich, and he grows rich—
only more slowly and modestly, perhaps,
than he expected; he dreams of marrying
his Rebecca and, even if he marries a Leah
instead, he ultimately finds in Leah his
Rebecca after all. He dreams of helping
to carry on and to accelerate the movement
of a vast, seething, progressive society, and
he actually does so. Ideals clinging so close
to nature are almost sure of fulfilment; the
American beams with a certain self-confidence and sense of mastery; he feels that
God and nature are working with him.

Idealism in the American accordingly
goes hand in hand with present contentment
and with foresight of what the future very
likely will actually bring. He is not a
revolutionist; he believes he is already on
the right track and moving towards an
excellent destiny. In revolutionists, on the
contrary, idealism is founded on dissatisfaction and expresses it. What exists seems
to them an absurd jumble of irrational
accidents and bad habits, and they want the
future to be based on reason and to be the
pellucid embodiment of all their maxims.
All their zeal is for something radically dif-

ferent from the actual and (if they only knew
it) from the possible; it is ideally simple,
and they love it and believe in it because
their nature craves it. They think life would
be set free by the destruction of all its organs.
They are therefore extreme idealists in the
region of hope, but not at all, as poets and
artists are, in the region of perception and
memory. In the atmosphere of civilised
life they miss all the refraction and all the
fragrance; so that in their conception of
actual things they are apt to be crude
realists; and their ignorance and inexperience of the moral world, unless it comes of
ill-luck, indicates their incapacity for education. Now incapacity for education, when
united with great inner vitality, is one root
of idealism. It is what condemns us all,
in the region of sense, to substitute perpetually what we are capable of imagining for
what things may be in themselves; it is
what condemns us, wherever it extends, to
think *a priori*; it is what keeps us bravely
and incorrigibly pursuing what we call the
good—that is, what would fulfil the demands
of our nature—however little provision the
fates may have made for it. But the want

of insight on the part of revolutionists
touching the past and the present infects
in an important particular their idealism
about the future; it renders their dreams
of the future unrealisable. For in human
beings—this may not be true of other
animals, more perfectly preformed—experience is necessary to pertinent and concrete
thinking; even our primitive instincts are
blind until they stumble upon some occasion
that solicits them; and they can be much
transformed or deranged by their first partial
satisfactions. Therefore a man who does
not idealise his experience, but idealises *a
priori*, is incapable of true prophecy; when
he dreams he raves, and the more he criticises
the less he helps. American idealism, on
the contrary, is nothing if not helpful,
nothing if not pertinent to practicable transformations; and when the American frets,
it is because whatever is useless and impertinent, be it idealism or inertia, irritates him;
for it frustrates the good results which he
sees might so easily have been obtained.

The American is wonderfully alive; and
his vitality, not having often found a suitable outlet, makes him appear agitated on

the surface; he is always letting off an unnecessarily loud blast of incidental steam. Yet his vitality is not superficial; it is inwardly prompted, and as sensitive and quick as a magnetic needle. He is inquisitive, and ready with an answer to any question that he may put to himself of his own accord; but if you try to pour instruction into him, on matters that do not touch his own spontaneous life, he shows the most extraordinary powers of resistance and oblivescence; so that he often is remarkably expert in some directions and surprisingly obtuse in others. He seems to bear lightly the sorrowful burden of human knowledge. In a word, he is young.

What sense is there in this feeling, which we all have, that the American is young? His country is blessed with as many elderly people as any other, and his descent from Adam, or from the Darwinian rival of Adam, cannot be shorter than that of his European cousins. Nor are his ideas always very fresh. Trite and rigid bits of morality and religion, with much seemly and antique political lore, remain axiomatic in him, as in the mind of a child; he may carry all this about with an unquestioning familiarity which does not comport understanding. To keep traditional sentiments in this way insulated and uncriticised is itself a sign of youth. A good young man is naturally conservative and loyal on all those subjects which his experience has not brought to a test ; advanced opinions on politics, marriage, or literature are comparatively rare in America ; they are left for the ladies to discuss, and usually to condemn, while the men get on with their work. In spite of what is old-fashioned in his more general ideas, the American is unmistakably young ; and this, I should say, for two reasons : one, that he is chiefly occupied with his immediate environment, and the other, that his reactions upon it are inwardly prompted, spontaneous, and full of vivacity and self-trust. His views are not yet lengthened ; his will is not yet broken or transformed. The present moment, however, in this, as in other things, may mark a great change in him ; he is perhaps now reaching his majority, and all I say may hardly apply to-day, and may not apply at all to-morrow. I speak of him as I have known him ; and whatever moral strength may accrue to him later, I am not sorry to have known him in his youth. The charm of youth, even when it is a little boisterous, lies in nearness to the impulses of nature, in a quicker and more obvious obedience to that pure, seminal principle which, having formed the body and its organs, always directs their movements, unless it is forced by vice or necessity to make them crooked, or to suspend them. Even under the inevitable crust of age the soul remains young, and, wherever it is able to break through, sprouts into something green and tender. We are all as young at heart as the most youthful American, but the seed in his case has fallen upon virgin soil, where it may spring up more bravely and with less respect for the giants of the wood. Peoples seem older when their perennial natural youth is encumbered with more possessions and prepossessions, and they are mindful of the many things they have lost or missed. The American is not mindful of them.

In America there is a tacit optimistic assumption about existence, to the effect that the more existence the better. The soulless critic 'might urge that quantity is only a physical category, implying no excellence, but' at best an abundance of opportunities both for good and for evil. Yet the young soul, being curious and hungry, views existence *a priori* under the form of the good ; its instinct to live implies a faith that most things it can become or see or do will be worth while. Respect for quantity is accordingly something more than the childish joy and wonder at bigness ; it is the fisherman's joy in a big haul, the good uses of which he can take for granted. Such optimism is amiable. Nature cannot afford that we should begin by being too calculating or wise, and she encourages us by the pleasure she attaches to our functions in advance of their fruits, and often in excess of them ; as the angler enjoys catching his fish more than eating it, and often, waiting patiently for the fish to bite, misses his own supper. The pioneer must devote himself to preparations ; he must work for the future, and it is healthy and dutiful of him to love his work for its own sake. At the same time, unless reference to an ultimate purpose is at least virtual in all his activities, he runs the

danger of becoming a living automaton,
vain and ignominious in its mechanical con-
stancy. Idealism about work can hide, an
intense materialism about life. Man, if he
is a rational being, cannot live by bread
alone nor be a labourer merely ; he must
eat and work in view of an ideal harmony
which overarches all his days, and which is
realised in the way they hang together, or in
some ideal issue which they have in common.
Otherwise, though his technical philosophy
may call itself idealism, he is a materialist in
morals ; he esteems things, and esteems
himself, for mechanical uses and energies.
Even sensualists, artists, and pleasure-lovers
are wiser than that, for though their idealism
may be desultory or corrupt, they attain
something ideal, and prize things only for
their living effects, moral though perhaps
fugitive. Sensation, when we do not take
it as a signal for action, but arrest and
peruse what it positively brings before us,
reveals something ideal—a colour, shape,
or sound ; and to dwell on these presences,
with no thought of their material significance,
is an æsthetic or dreamful idealism. To
pass from this idealism to the knowledge

of matter is a great intellectual advance, and goes with dominion over the world ; for in the practical arts the mind is adjusted to a larger object, with more depth and potentiality in it ; which is what makes people feel that the material world is real, as they call it, and that the ideal world is not. Certainly the material world is real ; for the philosophers who deny the existence of matter are like the critics who deny the existence of Homer. If there was never any Homer, there must have been a lot of other poets no less Homeric than he ; and if matter does not exist, a combination of other things exists which is just as material. But the intense reality of the material world would not prevent it from being a dreary waste in our eyes, or even an abyss of horror, if it brought forth no spiritual fruits. In fact, it does bring forth spiritual fruits, for otherwise we should not be here to find fault with it, and to set up our ideals over against it. Nature is material, but not materialistic ; it issues in life, and breeds all sorts of warm passions and idle beauties. And just as sympathy with the mechanical travail and turmoil of nature, apart from its spiritual fruits, is moral materialism, so the continual perception and love of these fruits is moral idealism—happiness in the presence of immaterial objects and harmonies, such as we envisage in affection, speculation, religion, and all the forms of the beautiful.

The circumstances of his life hitherto have necessarily driven the American into moral materialism ; for in his dealings with material things he can hardly stop to enjoy their sensible aspects, which are ideal, nor proceed at once to their ultimate uses, which are ideal too.   He is practical as against the poet, and worldly as against the clear philosopher or the saint.  The most striking expression of this materialism is usually supposed to be his love of the almighty dollar ; but that is a foreign and unintelligent view. The American talks about money, because that is the symbol and measure he has at hand for success, intelligence, and power ; but as to money itself he makes, loses, spends, and gives it away with a very light heart.  To my mind the most striking expression of his materialism is his singular preoccupation with quantity.  If, for instance, you visit Niagara Falls, you may

expect to hear how many cubic feet or metric
tons of water are precipitated per second
over the cataract; how many cities and
towns (with the number of their inhabitants)
derive light and motive power from it ; and
the annual value of the further industries
that might very well be carried on by the
same means, without visibly depleting the
world's greatest wonder or injuring the
tourist trade. That is what I confidently
expected to hear on arriving at the adjoining
town of Buffalo; but I was deceived. The
first thing I heard instead was that there
are more miles of asphalt pavement in Buffalo
than in any city in the world. Nor is this
insistence on quantity confined to men of
business. The President of Harvard College,
seeing me once by chance soon after the beginning of a term, inquired how my classes
were getting on; and when I replied that
I thought they were getting on well, that
my men seemed to be keen and intelligent, he stopped me as if I was about
to waste his time. "I meant," said he,
"*what is the number* of students in your
classes."

Here I think we may perceive that this

love of quantity often has a silent partner, which is diffidence as to quality. The democratic conscience recoils before anything that savours of privilege ; and lest it should concède an unmerited privilege to any pursuit or person, it reduces all things as far as possible to the common denominator of quantity. Numbers cannot lie : but if it came to comparing the ideal beauties of philosophy with those of Anglo-Saxon, who should decide ? All studies are good—why else have universities ?—but those must be most encouraged which attract the greatest number of students. Hence the President's question. Democratic faith, in its diffidence about quality, throws the reins of education upon the pupil's neck, as Don Quixote threw the reins on the neck of Rocinante, and bids his divine instinct choose its own way.

The American has never yet had to face the trials of Job. Great crises, like the Civil War, he has known how to surmount victoriously ; and now that he has surmounted a second great crisis victoriously, it is possible that he may relapse, as he did in the other case, into an apparently complete absorption in material enterprise and prosperity. But if serious and irremediable tribulation ever overtook him, what would his attitude be ? It is then that we should be able to discover whether materialism or idealism lies at the base of his character. Meantime his working mind is not without its holiday. He spreads humour pretty thick and even over the surface of conversation, and humour is one form of moral emancipation. He loves land-scape, he loves mankind, and he loves know-ledge ; and in music at least he finds an art which he unfeignedly enjoys. In music and landscape, in humour and kindness, he touches the ideal more truly, perhaps, than in his ponderous academic idealisms and busy religions ; for it is astonishing how much even religion in America (can it possibly be so in England ?) is a matter of meetings, building-funds, schools, charities, clubs, and picnics. To be poor in order to be simple, to produce less in order that the product may be more choice and beautiful, and may leave us less burdened with un-necessary duties and useless possessions—that is an ideal not articulate in the American mind ; yet here and there I seem to have heard a sigh after it, a groan at the perpetual incubus of business and shrill society. Significant witness to such aspirations is borne by those new forms of popular religion, not mere* variations on tradition, which have sprung up from the soil—revivalism, spiritualism, Christian Science, the New Thought. Whether or no we can tap, through these or other channels, some cosmic or inner energy not hitherto at the disposal of man (and there is nothing incredible in that), we certainly may try to remove friction and waste in the mere process of living; we may relax morbid strains, loosen suppressed instincts, iron out the creases of the soul, discipline ourselves into simplicity, sweetness, and peace. These religious movements are efforts toward such physiological economy and hygiene; and while they are thoroughly plebeian, with no great lights, and no idea of raising men from the most vulgar and humdrum worldly existence, yet they see the possibility of physical and moral health on that common plane, and pursue it. That is true morality. The dignities of various types of life or mind, like the gifts of various animals, are relative. The snob adores one type only, and the creatures supposed by him to illustrate it perfectly; or envies and hates them, which is just as snobbish. Veritable lovers of life, on the contrary, like Saint Francis or like Dickens, know that in every tenement of clay, with no matter what endowment or station, happiness and perfection are possible to the soul. There must be no brow-beating, with shouts of work or progress or revolution, any more than with threats of hell-fire. What does it profit a man to free the whole world if his soul is not free ? Moral freedom is not an artificial condition, because the ideal is the mother tongue of both the heart and the senses. All that is requisite is that we should pause in living to enjoy life, and should lift up our hearts to things that are pure goods in themselves, so that once to have found and loved them, whatever else may betide, may remain a happiness that nothing can sully. This natural idealism does not imply that we are immaterial, but only that we are animate and truly alive. When the senses are sharp, as they are in the American, they are already half liberated, already a joy in themselves; and when the heart is warm, like his, and eager to be just, its ideal destiny can hardly be doubtful. It will not be always merely pumping and working; time and its own pulses will lend it wings.

# CHAPTER VII

THE straits of Dover, which one may sometimes see across, have sufficed so to isolate England that it has never moved quite in step with the rest of Europe in politics, morals, or art. No wonder that the Atlantic Ocean, although it has favoured a mixed emigration and cheap intercourse, should have cut off America so effectually that all the people there, even those of Latin origin, have become curiously different from any kind of European. In vain are they reputed to have the same religions or to speak the same languages as their cousins in the old world; everything has changed its accent, spirit, and value. Flora and fauna have been intoxicated by that untouched soil and fresh tonic air, and by those vast spaces; in spite of their hereditary differences of species they have all acquired the same crude savour and defiant aspect. In comparison with their European prototypes they seem tough, meagre, bold, and ugly. In the United States, apart from the fact that most of the early colonists belonged to an exceptional type of Englishman, the scale and speed of life have made everything strangely un-English. There is cheeriness instead of doggedness, confidence instead of circumspection ; there is a desire to quizz and to dazzle rather than a fear of being mistaken or of being shocked ; there is a pervasive cordiality, exaggeration, and farcical humour; and in the presence of the Englishman, when by chance he turns up or is thought of, there is an invincible impatience and irritation that his point of view should be so fixed, his mind so literal, and the freight he carries so excessive (when you are sailing in ballast yourself), and that he should seem to take so little notice of changes in the wind to which you are nervously sensitive.

Nevertheless there is one gift or habit, native to England, that has not only been preserved in America unchanged, but has found there a more favourable atmosphere

O

in which to manifest its true nature—I mean the spirit of free co-operation. The root of it is free individuality, which is deeply seated in the English inner man; there is an indomitable instinct or mind in him which he perpetually consults and reveres, slow and embarrassed as his expression of it may be. But this free individuality in the Englishman is crossed and biased by a large residue of social servitude. The church and the aristocracy, entanglement in custom and privilege, mistrust and bitterness about particular grievances, warp the inner man and enlist him against his interests in alien causes; the straits of Dover were too narrow, the shadow of a hostile continent was too oppressive, the English sod was soaked with too many dews and cut by too many hedges, for each individual, being quite master of himself, to confront every other individual without fear or prejudice, and to unite with him in the free pursuit of whatever aims they might find that they had in common. Yet this slow co-operation of free men, this liberty in democracy—the only sort that America possesses or believes in—is wholly English in its personal basis, its reserve, its tenacity, its empiricism, its public spirit, and its assurance of its own rightness ; and it deserves to be called English always, to whatever countries it may spread.

The omnipresence in America of this spirit of co-operation, responsibility, and growth is very remarkable. Far from being neutral-ised by American dash and bravura, or lost in the opposite instincts of so many alien races, it seems to be adopted at once in the most mixed circles and in the most novel predicaments. In America social servitude is reduced to a minimum ; in fact we may almost say that it is reduced to subjecting children to their mothers and to a common public education, agencies that are absolutely indispensable to produce the individual and enable him to exercise his personal initiative effectually ; for after all, whatever meta-physical egotism may say, one cannot vote to be created. But once created, weaned, and taught to read and write, the young American can easily shoulder his knapsack and choose his own way in the world. He is as yet very little trammelled by want of opportunity, and he has no roots to speak of in place, class, or religion. Where indi-

viduality is so free, co-operation, when it is
justified, can be all the more quick and hearty.
Everywhere co-operation is taken for granted,
as something that no one would be so mean
or so short-sighted as to refuse. Together
with the will to work and to prosper, it is of
the essence of Americanism, and is accepted
as such by all the unkempt polyglot peoples
that turn to the new world with the pathetic
but manly purpose of beginning life on a new
principle. Every political body, every public
meeting, every club, or college, or athletic
team, is full of it. Out it comes whenever
there is an accident in the street or a division
in a church, or a great unexpected emergency
like the late war. The general instinct is to
run and help, to assume direction, to pull
through somehow by mutual adaptation, and
by seizing on the readiest practical measures
and working compromises. Each man joins
in and gives a helping hand, without a preconceived plan or a prior motive. Even the
leader, when he is a natural leader and not a
professional, has nothing up his sleeve to force
on the rest, in their obvious good-will and
mental blankness. All meet in a genuine
spirit of consultation, eager to persuade but

reàdy to be persuaded, with a cheery confidence in their average ability, when a point
comes up and is clearly put before them, to
decide it for the time being, and to move on.
It is implicitly agreed, in every case, that
dispûted questions shall be put to a vote,
and that the minority will loyally acquiesce
in the decision of the majority and build
henceforth upon it, without a thought of ever
retracting it.

Such a way of proceeding seems in America
a matter of course, because it is bred in the
bone, or imposed by that permeating social
contagion which is so irresistible in a natural
democracy. But if we consider human nature
at large and the practice of most nations, we
shall see that it is a very rare, wonderful, and
unstable convention. It implies a rather
unimaginative optimistic assumption that
at bottom all men's interests are similar and
compatible, and a rather heroic public spirit
—such that no special interest, in so far as
it has to be overruled, shall rebel and try
to maintain itself absolutely. In America
hitherto these conditions happen to have
been actually fulfilled in an unusual measure.
Interests have been very similar—to exploit

business opportunities and organise pu
services useful to all; and these sin
interests have been also compatible
harmonious. A neighbour, even a c
petitor, where the field is so large and
little pre-empted, has more often prove
resource than a danger. The rich h
helped the public more than they have flee
it, and they have been emulated more t
hated or served by the enterprising p
To abolish millionaires would have beer
dash one's own hopes. The most oppc
systems of religion and education could l
smilingly upon one another's prospcı
because the country could afford these su
ficial luxuries, having a constitutional reli;
and education of its own, which everyb
drank in unconsciously and which assı
the moral cohesion of the people. Impı
of reason and kindness, which are poter
in all men, under such circumstances
become effective; people can help one ano
with no great sacrifice to themselves,
minorities can dismiss their special p
without sorrow, and cheerfully follow
crowd down another road. It was becı
life in America was naturally more

operative and more plastic than in England
that the spirit of English liberty, which
demands co-operation and plasticity, could
appear there more boldly and universally
than it ever did at home.

English liberty is a method, not a goal.
It is related to the value of human life very
much as the police are related to public
morals or commerce to wealth ; and it is no
accident that the Anglo-Saxon race excels in
commerce and in the commercial as distinguished from the artistic side of industry,
and that having policed itself successfully
it is beginning to police the world at large.
It is all an eminence in temper, good-will,
reliability, accommodation. Probably some
other races, such as the Jews and Arabs,
make individually better merchants, more
shrewd, patient, and loving of their art.
Englishmen and Americans often seem to
miss or force opportunities, to play for quick
returns, or to settle down into ponderous
corporations ; for successful men they are
not particularly observant, constant, or
economical. But the superiority of the
Oriental is confined to his private craft; he
has not the spirit of partnership. In English

civilisation the individual is neutralised ; · it does not matter so much even in high places if he is rather stupid or rather cheap ; public spirit sustains him, and he becomes its instrument all the more readily, perhaps, for not being very distinguished or clear-headed in himself. The community prospers ; comfort and science, good manners and generous feelings are diffused among the people, without the aid of that foresight and cunning direction which sometimes give a temporary advantage to a rival system like the German. In the end, adaptation to the world at large, where so much is hidden and unintelligible, is only possible piecemeal, by groping with a genuine indetermination in one's aims. Its very looseness gives the English method its lien on the future. To dominate the world co-operation is better than policy, and empiricism safer than inspiration. Anglo-Saxon imperialism is unintended ; military conquests are incidental to it and often not maintained ; it subsists by a mechanical equilibrium of habits and interests, in which every colony, province, or protectorate has a different status. It has a commercial and missionary quality, and is essentially an

invitation to pull together—an invitation
which many nations may be incapable of
accepting or even of understanding, or which
they may deeply scorn, because it involves a
surrender of absolute liberty on their part ;
but whether accepted or rejected, it is an
offer of co-operation, a project for a limited
partnership, not a complete plan of life to be
imposed on anybody.

It is a wise instinct, in dealing with
foreigners or with material things (which
are foreigners to the mind), to limit oneself
in this way to establishing external relations,
partial mutual adjustments, with a great
residuum of independence and reserve ; if
you attempt more you will achieve less ;
your interpretations will become chimerical
and your regimen odious. So deep-seated
is this prudent instinct in the English nature
that it appears even at home ; most of the
concrete things which English genius has
produced are expedients. Its spiritual
treasures are hardly possessions, except as
character is a possession ; they are rather
a standard of life, a promise, an insurance.
English poetry and fiction form an exception ;
the very incoherence and artlessness which

they share with so much else that is English lend them an absolute value as an expression. They are the mirror and prattle of the inner man—a boyish spirit astray in the green earth it loves, rich in wonder, perplexity, valour, and faith, given to opinionated little prejudices, but withal sensitive and candid, and often laden, as in *Hamlet*, with exquisite music, tender humour, and tragic self-knowledge. But apart from the literature that simply utters the inner man, no one considering the English language, the English church, or English philosophy, or considering the common law and parliamentary government, would take them for perfect realisations of art or truth or an ideal polity. Institutions so jumbled and limping could never have been planned; they can never be transferred to another setting, or adopted bodily; but special circumstances and contrary currents have given them birth, and they are accepted and prized, where they are native, for keeping the door open to a great volume and variety of goods, at a moderate cost of danger and absurdity.

Of course no product of mind is *merely* an expedient; all are concomitantly expressions of temperament; there is something in their manner of being practical which is poetical and catches the rhythm of the heart. In this way anything foreign—and almost all the elements of civilisation in England and America are foreign—when it is adopted and acclimatised, takes on a native accent, especially on English lips; like the Latin words in the language, it becomes thoroughly English in texture. The English Bible, again, with its archaic homeliness and majesty, sets the mind brooding, not less than the old ballad most redolent of the native past and the native imagination; it fills the memory with solemn and pungent phrases; and this incidental spirit of poetry in which it comes to be clothed is a self-revelation perhaps more pertinent and welcome to the people than the alien revelations it professes to transmit. English law and parliaments, too, would be very unjustly judged if judged as practical contrivances only; they satisfy at the same time the moral interest people have in uttering and enforcing their feelings. These institutions are ceremonious, almost sacramental; they are instinct with a dramatic spirit deeper and more vital than their utility. Englishmen and Americans love debate; they love sitting round a table as if in consultation, even when the chairman has pulled the wires and settled everything beforehand, and when each of the participants listens only to his own remarks and votes according to his party. They love committees and commissions; they love public dinners with after-dinner speeches, those stammering compounds of facetiousness, platitude, and business. How distressing such speeches usually are, and how helplessly prolonged, does not escape anybody; yet every one demands them notwithstanding, because in pumping them up or sitting through them he feels he is leading the political life. A public man must show himself in public, even if not to advantage. The moral expressiveness of such institutions also helps to redeem their clumsy procedure; they would not be useful, nor work at all as they should, if people did not smack their lips over them and feel a profound pleasure in carrying them out. Without the English spirit, without the faculty of making themselves believe in public what they never feel in private, without the habit of clubbing together and facing facts, and feeling duty in a cautious, consultative, experimental way, English liberties forfeit their practical value ; as we see when they are extended to a volatile histrionic people like the Irish, or when a jury in France, instead of pronouncing simply on matters of fact and the credibility of witnesses, rushes in the heat of its patriotism to carry out, by its verdict, some political policy.

The practice of English liberty presupposes two things : that all concerned are fundamentally unanimous, and that each has a plastic nature, which he is willing to modify. If fundamental unanimity is lacking and all are not making in the same general direction, there can be no honest co-operation, no satisfying compromise. Every concession, under such circumstances, would be a temporary one, to be retracted at the first favourable moment ; it would amount to a mutilation of one's essential nature, a partial surrender of life, liberty, and happiness, tolerable for a time, perhaps, as the lesser of two evils, but involving a perpetual sullen opposition and hatred. To put things

to a vote, and to accept unreservedly the
decision of the majority, are points essential
to the English system; but they would be
absurd if fundamental agreement were not
presupposed.   Every decision that the
majority could conceivably arrive at must
leave it still possible for the minority to
live and prosper, even if not exactly in the
way they wished.   Were this not the case, a
decision by vote would be as alien a fatality
to any minority as the decree of a foreign
tyrant, and at every election the right of
rebellion would come into play.   In a hearty
and sound democracy all questions at issue
must be minor matters; fundamentals must
have been silently agreed upon and taken
for granted when the democracy arose.   To
leave a decision to the majority is like leaving
it to chance—a fatal procedure unless one is
willing to have it either way.   You must be
able to risk losing the toss; and if you do
you will acquiesce all the more readily in the
result, because, unless the winners cheated
at the game, they had no more influence
on it than yourself—namely none, or very
little.   You acquiesce in democracy on the
same conditions and for the same reasons,

and perhaps a little more cheerfully, because there is an infinitesimally better chance of winning on the average; but even then the enormity of the risk involved would be intolerable if anything of vital importance was at stake. It is therefore actually required that juries, whose decisions may really be of moment, should be unanimous; and parliaments and elections are never more satisfactory than when a wave of national feeling runs through them and there is no longer any minority nor any need of voting.

Free government works well in proportion as government is superfluous. That most parliamentary measures should be trivial or technical, and really devised and debated only in government offices, and that government in America should so long have been carried on in the shade, by persons of no name or dignity, is no anomaly. On the contrary, like the good fortune of those who never hear of the police, it is all a sign that co-operative liberty is working well and rendering overt government unnecessary. Sometimes kinship and opportunity carry a whole nation before the wind; but this

happy unison belongs rather to the dawn of
national life, when similar tasks absorb all
individual energies.   If it is to be maintained
after lines of moral cleavage appear, and is
to be compatible with variety and distinction
of character, all further developments must
be democratically controlled and must remain, as it were, in a state of fusion.   Variety
and distinction must not become arbitrary
and irresponsible.   They must take directions that will not mar the general harmony,
and no interest must be carried so far as to
lose sight of the rest.   Science and art, in
such a vital democracy, should remain popular, helpful, bracing ;   religion should be
broadly national and in the spirit of the
times.   The variety and distinction allowed
must be only variety and distinction of
service.   If they ever became a real distinction and variety of life, if they arrogated to
themselves an absolute liberty, they would
shatter the unity of the democratic spirit
and destroy its moral authority.

The levelling tendency of English liberty
(inevitable if plastic natures are to co-operate
and to make permanent concessions to one
another's instincts) comes out more clearly

in America than in England itself. In England there are still castles and rural retreats, there are still social islands within the Island, where special classes may nurse particular allegiances. America is all one prairie, swept by a universal tornado. Although it has always thought itself in an eminent sense the land of freedom, even when it was covered with slaves, there is no country in which people live under more overpowering compulsions. The prohibitions, although important and growing, are not yet, perhaps, so many or so blatant as in some other countries; but prohibitions are less galling than compulsions. What can be forbidden specifically—bigamy, for instance, or heresy—may be avoided by a prudent man without renouncing the whole movement of life and mind which, if carried beyond a certain point, would end in those trespasses against convention. He can indulge in hypothesis or gallantry without falling foul of the positive law, which indeed may even stimulate his interest and ingenuity by suggesting some indirect means of satisfaction. On the other hand, what is exacted cuts deeper; it creates habits which overlay nature, and every faculty is atrophied that does not conform with them. If, for instance, I am compelled to be in an office (and up to business, too) from early morning .to late afternoon, with long journeys in thundering and sweltering trains before and after and a flying shot at a quick lunch between, I am caught and held both in soul and body; and except for the freedom to work and to rise by that work—which may be very interesting in itself—I am not suffered to exist morally at all. My evenings will be drowsy, my Sundays tedious, and after a few days' holiday I shall be wishing to get back to business. Here is as narrow a path left open to freedom as is left open in a monastic establishment, where bell and book keep your attention fixed at all hours upon the hard work of salvation—an infinite vista, certainly, if your soul was not made to look another way. Those, too, who may escape this crushing routine—the invalids, the ladies, the fops—are none the less prevented by it from doing anything else with success or with a good conscience; the bubbles also must swim with the stream. Even what is best in American life is compulsory—the idealism, the zeal, the beautiful happy unison of its great moments. You must wave, you must cheer, you must push with the irresistible crowd; otherwise you will feel like a traitor, a soulless outcast, a deserted ship high and dry on the shore. In America there is but one way of being saved, though it is not peculiar to any of the official religions, which themselves must silently conform to the national orthodoxy, or else become impotent and merely ornamental. This national faith and morality are vague in idea, but inexorable in spirit; they are the gospel of work and the belief in progress. By them, in a country where all men are free, every man finds that what most matters has been settled for him beforehand.

Nevertheless, American life *is* free as a whole, because it is mobile, because every atom that swims in it has a momentum of its own which is felt and respected throughout the mass, like the weight of an atom in the solar system, even if the deflection it may cause is infinitesimal. In temper America is docile and not at all tyrannical; it has not predetermined its career, and its

merciless momentum is a passive resultant.
Like some Mississippi or Niagara, it rolls
its * myriad drops gently onward, being
but the suction and pressure which they
exercise on one another. Any tremulous
thought or playful experiment anywhere
may be a first symptom of great changes,
and may seem to precipitate the cataract
in a new direction. Any snowflake in a
boy's sky may become the centre for his
*boule de neige,* his prodigious fortune; but
the monster will melt as easily as it grew,
and leaves nobody poorer for having existed.
In America there is duty everywhere, but
everywhere also there is light. I do not
mean superior understanding or even moder-
ately wide knowledge, but openness to light,
an evident joy in seeing things clearly and
doing them briskly, which would amount to
a veritable triumph of art and reason if the
affairs in which it came into play were
central and important. The American may
give an exorbitant value to subsidiary things,
but his error comes of haste in praising
what he possesses, and trusting the first
praises he hears. He can detect sharp
practices, because he is capable of them,

but vanity or wickedness in the ultimate
aims of a man, including himself, he cannot
detect, because he is ingenuous in that
sphere. He thinks life splendid and blame-
less, without stopping to consider how far
folly and malice may be inherent in it. He
feels that he himself has nothing to dread,
nothing to hide or apologise for; and if he
is arrogant in his ignorance, there is often
a twinkle in his eye when he is most boastful. Perhaps he suspects that he is making
a fool of himself, and he challenges the
world to prove it; and his innocence is
quickly gone when he is once convinced that
it exists. Accordingly the American orthodoxy, though imperious, is not unyielding.
It has a keener sense for destiny than for
policy. It is confident of a happy and
triumphant future, which it would be shame-
ful in any man to refuse to work for and to
share; but it cannot prefigure what that
bright future is to be. While it works
feverishly in outward matters, inwardly it
only watches and waits; and it feels tenderly
towards the unexpressed impulses in its
bosom, like a mother towards her unborn
young.

There is a mystical conviction, expressed in Anglo-Saxon life and philosophy, that our labours, even when they end in failure, contribute to some ulterior achievement in which it is well they should be submerged. This Anglo-Saxon piety, in the form of trust and adaptability, reaches somewhat the same insight that more speculative religions have reached through asceticism, the insight that we must renounce our wills and deny ourselves. But to have a will remains essential to animals, and having a will we must kick against the pricks, even if philosophy thinks it foolish of us. The spirit in which parties and nations beyond the pale of English liberty confront one another is not motherly nor brotherly nor Christian. Their valorousness and morality consist in their indomitable egotism. The liberty they want is absolute liberty, a desire which is quite primitive. It may be identified with the love of life which animates all creation, or with the pursuit of happiness which all men would be engaged in if they were rational. Indeed, it might even be identified with the first law of motion, that all bodies, if left free, persevere in that state of rest, or of motion in a straight line, in which they happen to find themselves. The enemies of this primitive freedom are all such external forces as make it deviate from the course it is in the habit of taking or is inclined to take; and when people begin to reflect upon their condition, they protest against this alien tyranny, and contrast in fancy what they would do if they were free with what under duress they are actually doing. All human struggles are inspired by what, in this sense, is the love of freedom. Even craving for power and possessions may be regarded as the love of a free life on a larger scale, for which more instruments and resources are needed. The apologists of absolute will are not slow, for instance, to tell us that Germany in her laborious ambitions has been pursuing the highest form of freedom, which can be attained only by organising all the resources of the world, and the souls of all subsidiary nations, around one luminous centre of direction and self-consciousness, such as the Prussian government was eminently fitted to furnish. Freedom to exercise absolute will methodically seems to them much better than

English liberty, because it knows what it
wants, pursues it intelligently, and does not
rely for success on some measure of goodness
in mankind at large. English liberty is so
trustful! It moves by a series of checks,
mutual concessions, and limited satisfactions;
it counts on chivalry, sportsmanship, brotherly
love, and on that rarest and least lucrative of
virtues, fair-mindedness : it is a broad-based,
stupid, blind adventure, groping towards an
unknown goal. Who but an Englishman
would think of such a thing! A fanatic, a
poet, a doctrinaire, a dilettante — any one
who has a fixed aim and clear passions—
will not relish English liberty. It will seem
bitter irony to him to give the name of
liberty to something so muffled, exacting,
and oppressive. In fact English liberty is
a positive infringement and surrender of the
freedom most fought for and most praised in
the past. It makes impossible the sort of
liberty for which the Spartans died at
Thermopylæ, or the Christian martyrs in the
arena, or the Protestant reformers at the
stake ; for these people all died because
they would not co-operate, because they were
not plastic and would never consent to lead

the life dear or at least customary to other men. They insisted on being utterly different and independent and inflexible in their chosen systems, and aspired either to destroy the society round them or at least to insulate themselves in the midst of it, and live a jealous, private, unstained life of their own within their city walls or mystical conclaves. Any one who passionately loves his particular country or passionately believes in his particular religion cannot be content with less liberty or more democracy than that ; he must be free to live absolutely according to his ideal, and no hostile votes, no alien interests, must call on him to deviate from it by one iota. Such was the claim to religious liberty which has played so large a part in the revolutions and divisions of the western world. Every new heresy professed to be orthodoxy itself, purified and restored ; and woe to all backsliders from the reformed faith ! Even the popes, without thinking to be ironical, have often raised a wail for liberty. Such too was the aspiration of those mediæval cities and barons who fought for their liberties and rights. Such was the aspiration even of the American declaration of independence and the American constitution : cast-iron documents, if only the spirit of co-operative English liberty had not been there to expand, embosom, soften, or transform them. So the French revolution and the Russian one of to-day have aimed at establishing society once for all on some eternally just principle, and at abolishing all traditions, interests, faiths, and even words that did not belong to their system. Liberty, for all these pensive or rabid apostles of liberty, meant liberty for themselves to be just so, and to remain just so for ever, together with the most vehement defiance of anybody who might ask them, for the sake of harmony, to be a little different. They summoned every man to become free in exactly their own fashion, or have his head cut off.

Of course, to many an individual, life even in any such free city or free church, fiercely jealous of its political independence and moral purity, would prove to be a grievous servitude ; and there has always been a sprinkling of rebels and martyrs and scornful philosophers protesting and fuming against their ultra-independent and nothing-if-not-

protesting sects. To co-operate with anybody seems to these *esprits forts* contamina-
tion, so sensitive are they to any deviation
from the true north which their compass
might suffer through the neighbourhood of
any human magnet. If it is a weakness to
be subject to influence, it is an imprudence
to expose oneself to it; and to be subject
to influence seems ignominious to any one
whose inward monitor is perfectly articulate
and determined. A certain vagueness of
soul, together with a great gregariousness and
tendency to be moulded by example and by
prevalent opinion, is requisite for feeling free
under English liberty. You must find the
majority right enough to live with; you
must give up lost causes; you must be willing to put your favourite notions to sleep in
the family cradle of convention. Enthusiasts
for democracy, peace, and a league of nations
should not deceive themselves; they are not
everybody's friends; they are the enemies
of what is deepest and most primitive in
everybody. They inspire undying hatred in
every untamable people and every absolute
soul.

It is in the nature of wild animal life to

be ferocious or patient, and in either case heroic and uncompromising. It is inevitable, in the beginning, that each person or faction should come into the lists to serve some express interest, which in itself may be perfectly noble and generous. But these interests are posited alone and in all their ultimate consequences. The parties meet, however diplomatic their procedure, as buyers and sellers bargain in primitive markets. Each has a fixed programme or, as he perhaps calls it, an ideal; and when he has got as much as he can get to-day, he will return to the charge to-morrow, with absolutely unchanged purpose. All opposed parties he regards as sheer enemies to be beaten down, driven off, and ultimately converted or destroyed. Meantime he practises political craft, of which the climax is war; a craft not confined to priests, though they are good at it, but common to every missionary, agitator, and philosophical politician who operates in view of some vested interest or inflexible plan, in the very un-English spirit of intrigue, cajolery, eloquence, and dissimulation. His art is to worm his way forward, using people's passions to further

his own ends, carrying them off their feet in
a wave of enthusiasm, when that is feasible,
and when it is not, recommending his cause
by insidious half-measures, flattery of private
interests, confidence-tricks, and amiable suggestions, until he has put his entangled
victims in his pocket; or when he feels
strong enough, brow-beating and intimidat-
ing them into silence. Such is the inevitable
practice of every prophet who heralds an
absolute system, political or religious, and
who pursues the unqualified domination of
principles which he thinks right in themselves and of a will which is self-justified
and irresponsible.

Why, we may ask, are people so ready to
set up absolute claims, when their resources
are obviously so limited that permanent
success is impossible, and their will itself, in
reality, is so fragile that it abandons each of
its dreams even before it learns that it cannot
be realised ? The reason is that the feebler,
more ignorant, and more childlike an impulse
is, the less it can restrain itself or surrender
a part of its desire in order the better to
attain the rest. In most nations and most
philosophies the intellect is rushed ; it is

swept forward and enamoured by the first
glimpses it gets of anything good. The
dogmas thus precipitated seem to relieve
the will of all risks and to guarantee its enterprises ; whereas in fact they are rendering
every peril tragic by blinding us to it, and
every vain hope incorrigible. A happy shyness in the English mind, a certain torpor
and lateness in its utterance, have largely
saved it from this calamity, and just because
it is not brilliant it is safe. Being reticent,
it remains fertile ; being vague in its destina-
tion, it can turn at each corner down the
most inviting road. In this race the intellect
has chosen the part of prudence, leaving
courage to the will, where courage is indispensable. How much more becoming and
fortunate is this balance of faculties for an
earthly being than an intellect that scales
the heavens, refuting and proving everything,
while the will dares to attempt and to reform
nothing, but fritters itself away in sloth,
petty malice, and irony ! In the English
character modesty and boldness appear in
the right places and in a just measure.
Manliness ventures to act without pretending
to be sure of the issue ; it does not cry that

all is sure, in order to cover up the mortal perils of finitude; and manliness has its reward in the joys of exploration and comradeship.

It is this massive malleable character, this vigorous moral youth, that renders co-operation possible and progressive. When interests are fully articulate and fixed, co-operation is a sort of mathematical problem; up to a certain precise limit, people can obviously help one another by summing their efforts, like sailors pulling at a rope, or by a division of labour; they can obviously help one another when thereby they are helping themselves. But beyond that, there can be nothing but mutual indifference or eternal hostility. This is the old way of the world. Most of the lower animals, although they run through surprising transformations during their growth, seem to reach maturity by a predetermined method and in a predeter-mined form. Nature does everything for them and experience nothing, and they live or die, as the case may be, true to their innate character. Mankind, on the contrary, and especially the English races, seem to reach physical maturity still morally im-

mature; they need to be finished by education, experience, external influences. What
so often spoils other creatures improves them.
If left to themselves and untrained, they
remain all their lives stupid and coarse,
with no natural joy but drunkenness; but
nurseries and schools and churches and social
conventions can turn them into the most
refined and exquisite of men, and admirably
intelligent too, in a cautious and special
fashion. They may never become, for all
their pains, so agile, graceful, and sure as
many an animal or *a priori* man is without
trouble, but they acquire more representa-
tive minds and a greater range of material
knowledge. Such completion, in the open
air, of characters only half-formed in the
womb may go on in some chance direction,
or it may go on in the direction of a greater
social harmony, that is, in whatever direction
is suggested to each man by the suasion of
his neighbours. Society is a second mother
to these souls; and the instincts of many
animals would remain inchoate if the great
instinct of imitation did not intervene and
enable them to learn by example. Develop-
ment in this case involves assimilation;

characters are moulded by contagion and
educated by democracy. The sphere of
unanimity tends to grow larger, and to
reduce the margin of diversity to insig-
nificance. The result is an ever-increasing
moral unison, which is the simplest form of
moral harmony and emotionally the most
coercive.

Democracy is often mentioned in the same
breath with liberty, as if they meant the
same thing; and both are sometimes identified with the sort of elective government that
prevails in Great Britain and the United
States. But just as English liberty seems
servitude to some people because it requires
them to co-operate, to submit to the majority,
and to grow like them, so English democracy
seems tyranny to the wayward masses,
because it is constitutional, historical, and
sacred, narrowing down the power of any
group of people at any time to voting for one
of two or three candidates for office, or to
saying yes or no to some specific proposal—
both the proposals and the candidates being
set before them by an invisible agency; and
fate was never more inexorable or blinder
than is the grinding of this ponderous political

Q

mill, where routine, nepotism, pique, and
swagger, with love of office and money, turn
all the wheels.  And the worst of it is that
the revolutionary parties that oppose this
historical machine repeat all its abuses, or
even aggravate them.  It would be well if
people in England and America woke up to
the fact that it is in the name of natural
liberty and direct democracy that enemies
both within and without are already rising
up against their democracy and their liberty.
Just as the Papacy once threatened English
liberties, because it would maintain one
inflexible international religion over all men,
so now an international democracy of the
disinherited many, led by the disinherited
few, threatens English liberties again, since
it would abolish those private interests which
are the factors in any co-operation, and
would reduce everybody to forced member-
ship and forced service in one universal flock,
without property, family, country, or religion.
That life under such a system might have its
comforts, its arts, and its atomic liberties, is
certain, just as under the Catholic system it
had its virtues and consolations ; but both
systems presuppose the universality of a type

of human nature which is not English, and perhaps not human.

The great advantage of English liberty is that it is in harmony with the nature of things; and when living beings have managed to adapt their habits to the nature of things, they have entered the path of health and wisdom. No doubt the living will is essentially absolute, both at the top and at the bottom, in the ferocious animal and in the rapt spirit; but it is absolute even then only in its deliverance, in what it asserts or demands; nothing can be less absolute or more precarious than the living will in its existence. A living will is the flexible voice of a thousand submerged impulses, of which now one and now another comes to the surface; it is responsive, without knowing it, to a complex forgotten past and a changing, unexplored environment. The will is a mass of passions; when it sets up absolute claims it is both tragic and ridiculous. It may be ready to be a martyr, but it will have to be one. Martyrs are heroic; but unless they have the nature of things on their side and their cause can be victorious, their heroism is like that of criminals and madmen, interesting dramatically but morally detestable. Madmen and criminals, like other martyrs, appeal to the popular imagination, because in each of us there is a little absolute will, or a colony of little absolute wills, aching to be criminal, mad, and heroic. Yet the equilibrium by which we exist if we are sane, and which we call reason, keeps these rebellious dreams under; if they run wild, we are lost. Reason is a harmony; and it has been reputed by egotistical philosophers to rule the world (in which unreason of every sort is fundamental and rampant), because when harmony between men and nature supervenes at any place or in any measure, the world becomes intelligible and safe, and philosophers are able to live in it. The passions, even in a rational society, remain the elements of life, but under mutual control, and the life of reason, like English liberty, is a perpetual compromise. Absolute liberty, on the contrary, is impracticable; it is a foolish challenge thrown by a new-born insect buzzing against the universe; it is incompatible with more than one pulse of life. All the declarations of independence in the world will not render anybody really independent. You may disregard your environment, you cannot escape it; and your disregard of it will bring you moral empoverishment and some day unpleasant surprises. Even Robinson Crusoe—whom offended America once tried to imitate—lived on what he had saved from the wreck, on footprints and distant hopes. Liberty to be left alone, not interfered with and not helped, is not English liberty. It is the primeval desire of every wild animal or barbarous tribe or jealous city or religion, claiming to live and to tramp through the world in its own sweet way. These combative organisms, however, have only such strength as the opposite principle of co-operation lends them inwardly; and the more liberty they assume in foreign affairs the less liberty their members can enjoy at home. At home they must then have organisation at all costs, like ancient Sparta and modern Germany; and even if the restraints so imposed are not irksome and there is spontaneous unison and enthusiasm in the people, the basis of such a local harmony will soon prove too narrow. Nations and religions will run up against one another, against change, against science, against all the realities they had never reckoned with ; and more or less painfully they will dissolve. And it will not be a normal and fruitful dissolution, like that of a man who leaves children and heirs. It will be the end of that evolution, the choking of that ideal in the sand.

This collapse of fierce liberty is no ordinary mutation, such as time brings sooner or later to everything that exists, when the circumstances that sustained it in being no longer prevail. It is a deep tragedy, because the narrower passions and swifter harmonies are more beautiful and perfect than the chaos or the dull broad equilibrium that may take their place. Co-operative life is reasonable and long-winded ; but it always remains imperfect itself, while it somewhat smothers the impulses that enter into it. Absolute liberty created these elements ; inspiration, free intelligence, uncompromising conviction, a particular home and breeding-ground, were requisite to give them birth. Nothing good could arise for co-operation to diffuse or to qualify unless first there had been complete liberty for the artist and an uncontaminated

perfection in his work. Reason and the
principle of English liberty have no 'creative
afflatus; they presuppose spontaneity and
yet they half stifle it; and they can rest in no
form of perfection, because they must remain
plastic and continually invite amendments,
in order to continue broadly adjusted to an
infinite moving world. Their work is accordingly like those cathedrals at which many
successive ages have laboured, each in its
own style. We may regret, sometimes, that
some one design could not have been carried
out in its purity, and yet all these secular
accretions have a wonderful eloquence; a
common piety and love of beauty have
inspired them; age has fused them and
softened their incongruities; and an in-
expressible magic seems to hang about the
composite pile, as if God and man breathed
deeply within it. It is a harmony woven
out of accidents, like every work of time and
nature, and all the more profound and fertile
because no mind could ever have designed it.
Some such natural structure, formed and
reformed by circumstances, is the requisite
matrix and home for every moral being.

Accordingly there seems to have been

sober sense and even severe thought behind
the rant of Webster when he cried, "Liberty
*and* Union, now and for ever, one and in-
separable ! " because if for the sake of liberty
you abandon union and resist a mutual
adaptation of purposes which might cripple
each of them, your liberty loses its massive-
ness, its plasticity, its power to survive
change ; it ceases to be tentative and human
in order to become animal and absolute.
Nature must always produce little irresponsible passions that will try to rule her,
but she can never crown any one of them
with more than a theatrical success ; the
wrecks of absolute empires, communisms,
and religions are there to prove it. But
English liberty, because it is co-operative,
because it calls only for a partial and shifting
unanimity among living men, may last
indefinitely, and can enlist every reasonable
man and nation in its service. This is the
best heritage of America, richer than its virgin
continents, which it draws from the temperate
and manly spirit of England. Certainly
absolute freedom would be more beautiful
if we were birds or poets ; but co-operation
and a loving sacrifice of a part of ourselves—

or even of the whole, save the love in us—
are beautiful too, if we are men living together.
Absolute liberty and English liberty are incompatible, and mankind must make a
painful and a brave choice between them.
The necessity of rejecting and destroying
some things that are beautiful is the deepest
curse of existence.

THE END

*Printed in Great Britain by R. & R. CLARK, LIMITED, Edinburgh.*

# REALISM

BY

## ARTHUR McDOWALL

FELLOW OF ALL SOULS COLLEGE, OXFORD

### 10s. 6d. net.

"Mr. McDowall's book is an attempt to discover whether there is any fundamental identity between realism in art and realism in philosophy. . . . When the ideas on both sides are still so chaotic, it would be unreasonable for any one student to hope to effect a final settlement between them ; he does well if he manages to clear some of the debatable ground and stimulate other hunters to follow in his tracks ; and in this Mr. McDowall has certainly succeeded. . . . He has no flabbiness of thought, and, while he does not toil after epigram, he is never afraid of bringing his argument to a point."—*Spectator.*

∽

"The deeply interesting book that Mr. McDowall has written upon Realism in art and thought has its value both as an exposition and a starting-point. . . . He reveals in literary criticism a rare and welcome candour of thought. . . . Reading of such a book as 'Realism' can act only as a reassurance and a stimulus. The book is a tonic and an encouragement. It is full of thought and sympathy."—FRANK SWINNERTON in the *Outlook.*

∽

"Here is beyond the shadow of a doubt a valuable book. . . . The portion devoted to the 'new realism' of philosophy is as stimulating as his purely aesthetic speculations . . . the scrupulous generosity characteristic of his whole inquiry."—*Times Literary Supplement.*

∽

"Out of the confusion created by those to whom terms of philosophy and aesthetics are mere catchwords, there now and then arises a voice raised in the praiseworthy effort to analyse and to attach some meaning to the labels used. Mr. McDowall's attempt to perform this service for 'realism' is most welcome. . . . The delightful and lucid style of the work . . . the fascinating store of examples from every branch of art."—*Cambridge Magazine.*

CONSTABLE AND COMPANY LIMITED.

# THE ARCHITECTURE
# OF HUMANISM

## STUDY IN THE HISTORY OF TASTE

BY

## GEOFFREY SCOTT

### 7s. 6d. net.

"Mr. Scott's profound and brilliant book. . . . He unites to a taste perhaps surer and more discriminating than Pater's a critical erudition and a mature philosophy that were not his. . . . There would be much more to say of this important and stimulating book, which marks a date in the criticism, not merely of Architecture, but of the aesthetic phenomenon in general. . . . Mr. Scott is an authentic Humanist philosopher; as a philosopher I can give him no higher praise."—ALGAR THOROLD in the *Morning Post*.

∽

"One of the best things about Mr. Scott's book is the steady poise it maintains through very intricate discussions. Penetration of a fallacy does not satisfy him; he is determined to see how the fallacy grew. . . . Mr. Scott's brilliantly lucid application to Architecture [of the theory of empathy]."—LANCELLES ABERCROMBIE in the *Manchester Guardian*.

∽

"This brilliant and discriminating book. . . . It would give an incomplete idea of the book to leave it without alluding to his gift for vivid pen-drawing and happy definition."—*Times Literary Supplement*.

∽

"Mr. Scott's brilliant essay in defence of Renaissance architecture has not convinced us, but we have had so much pleasure in the reading of it that we can forgive him certain sophistries for the sake of the original and attractive qualities of his matter and style. . . . Books such as this are all too rare. Mr. Scott has something to say and the ability to express himself."—*Westminster Gazette*.

## CONSTABLE AND COMPANY LIMITED.

CPSIA information can be obtained
at www.ICGtesting.com
Printed in the USA
LVHW111300260720
661563LV00001B/106

9 781406 716658